9789645783035

Barnes / US Imperialism Has Lost the Cold

Farsi

Praise for *Stereophonic*

"A fly-on-the-wall study of how people both need and viciously destroy each other, *Stereophonic* is a fiery family drama, as electrifying as any since *Who's Afraid of Virginia Woolf?* Its real-time dissection of making music—a collaboration between flawed, gifted artists wrangled into unison—is ingeniously entertaining and an incisive meta commentary on the nature of art. The play is a staggering achievement, and already feels like a must-see American classic." —NAVEEN KUMAR, *NEW YORK TIMES*

"David Adjmi's high-definition group portrait of musicians and engineers creating and cracking is a long, luxurious beauty. Adjmi has worked on this play for a long time (almost a decade), and his devotion and insane attention to detail has yielded a dense and novelistic weave with the uncanny heft of observed life. Does *Stereophonic* rock? It does, hard. Instant classic."

—DAVID COTE, *OBSERVER*

"Masterful . . . A three-hour dissection of ego, insecurity, and the messy, messed-up gorgeousness of the creative process . . . What a brilliant piece of must-see Broadway."

—CHRIS JONES, *CHICAGO TRIBUNE*

"The best play I've seen in years." —ZACK CHRISTENSON, *SPECTATOR*

"A three-hour play about an unnamed 1970s band recording an album, set entirely in the recording studio: That's, essentially, the elevator pitch for *Stereophonic*, which just opened on Broadway after a sold-out ten-week run at Playwrights Horizons in late 2023. But that doesn't even begin to describe the genius on display at the Golden Theatre."

—MELISSA ROSE BERNARDO, *NEW YORK STAGE REVIEW*

"*Stereophonic* proceeds like a fictionalized documentary, a behind-the-scenes view of what it costs to make lasting art. But this detailed study is itself a work of pure imagination, a choreographic poem in which the messy minutiae of collaboration is coordinated in theatrical space to lay bare the dirty human secrets of artistic creation." —CHARLES MCNULTY, *LOS ANGELES TIMES*

"*Stereophonic* is the real thing. It's clear-eyed about the pitfalls of collaboration, interested as much in the hurt feelings that go into songwriting as effects of dust on a soundboard . . . In the rare, beautiful moments when everything falls into place and the band arrives at a nearly perfect take, the effect is overwhelming."

—Jackson McHenry, *Vulture*

"One of the most thrilling pieces of theater in years, *Stereophonic* is a hypernaturalistic meditation on the thrill, and also the danger, of collaborating on art—the compromises, the egos, and the joys. It's an ode not just to the music business but perhaps to the theater world, too." —Mark Kennedy, *Associated Press*

"Riveting . . . An intimately epic behind-the-music drama . . . With sharp-eyed but open-hearted insight and humor, Adjmi builds scene upon scene, teasing out relationships in well-observed exchanges among two or three characters and then feeding them into a complex mix. And all the layers come together beautifully."

—Adam Feldman, *Time Out New York*

"You know a piece of theater has done something right when, many days later, it is still provoking pin-pricks of intrigue, revelation, and mystery in one's mind. Both the act of making the music the fictional band does in front of us, and also the work of art we have seen, is a unique act of creation about the act of creation. *Stereophonic*, in this sense, is an impressive double artistic achievement . . . A must-experience, rather than simply a must-see."

—Tim Teeman, *Daily Beast*

"A searing, almost documentary-like portrait of what transpires when artistic expression ends up on a collision course with controlling perfectionism, and whether relationships inside the studio walls can survive complications from outside it—and vice versa. *Stereophonic* is a riveting, painful, funny, intense, toe-tapping journey, and the end result can best be described as solid gold."

—Dalton Ross, *Entertainment Weekly*

"*Stereophonic*'s title, delightfully apt, alludes not only to the multidirectional sound channeling which had become the norm in that era, but to its wonderfully Altman-esque style of overlapping dialogue and naturalism . . . It feels like listening to a favorite LP: rich in content, dynamic in production, wondrous in effect, and worth playing over and over." —JUAN A. RAMIREZ, *THEATRELY*

"Art is not easy, and *Stereophonic* painstakingly reveals how so much time, labor, love, loss, and literal tape it can take to make that art happen. Refreshing, eye-opening, and honest, Adjmi's vision of this rock-and-roll world includes a bag of blow and plenty of sex, but in this recording studio it is more about the screaming, fights, sleepless nights, anguish, and fear. We get this beautiful and agonizing glimpse of the risks, luck, and talent that come together in an alchemical mix when making an album. It is a rare gift, and so is this play." —NICOLE SERRATORE, *EXEUNT*

"Like a vinyl classic being removed from its gatefold cover inch by inch, *Stereophonic* slowly reveals its complexity, sharing the highs that come from working collectively to make great art and the spiraling lows of a shattered union. What makes it so riveting—in a dual-channel way reflected in the title—is that in addition to the rich characterizations and rocky group dynamics, we get incredible specificity in the world Adjmi has conjured . . . By the time the play ends, its searing emotional heft creeps up and grabs you by the throat. It's a chart topper." —DAVID ROONEY, *HOLLYWOOD REPORTER*

"*Stereophonic* is a unique and singular exploration of the passion and torment that comes with making art that passes the test of time, and I have little doubt that this play will, too."

—DAVID GORDON, *THEATERMANIA*

"*Stereophonic* is an allegory of industry greed and artistry. But the play, as a work itself, serves as a triumphant example of what happens when art has the time to develop, to hone in on the basics of craft, character, and spirit. Adjmi has carved a compelling tragedy on power, art-making, and the derided women propping up male 'geniuses.'" —GLORIA OLADIPO, *GUARDIAN*

"An electrifying evening of music creation as one would imagine happened in iconic recording studios, David Adjmi has struck platinum with his astounding *Stereophonic*. Adjmi's dialogue and complications are so organically constructed, intimate and authentic, that the action never languishes. A *tour de force*."

—CAROLE DI TOSTI, *THEATER PIZZAZZ*

"*Stereophonic* compels as a poignant character study and needle-sharp comedy. Across a luxurious three hours—to be sure, the action never drags—relationships crumble, friendships are betrayed, and nerve endings are given a thorough flaying. As songs are recorded and rerecorded, psychodramas are unleashed. Art, it seems, can be forged even in a crucible riddled with cracks."

—David Barbour, *Lighting and Sound America*

"*Stereophonic* is an ambitious undertaking, bringing an epic-length story in a logistically complicated setting to the stage in a way that feels inviting to both those who know the recording world well and those who have never set foot in a studio. Adjmi has a lot to say about the ugly, often mundane aspects of the creative act versus the polished sheen of the finished product—the artifice of art itself."

—Clive Young, *Mix*

"In *Stereophonic*, we watch people cooperate at making art, no matter the cost to themselves. As they overthink and argue about each aspect of their music, from tempos that sound wrong to vocals that come out just right, their relationships come apart as their musical career comes together . . . Adjmi has an ear for natural dialogue and the cadence of overlapping emotion as well as speech. He uses it well, letting the dual spaces of the set and the convenient microphones do the work. You feel like you're eavesdropping on real people. People who make music. People who make art."

—Julia Polinsky, *Theater Scene*

"*Stereophonic* is a play about the rise of a mythic rock band, but from the inside, it's a play about a broken coffee machine, a fleeting attempt at sobriety, or the stray rattle of a snare drum. Adjmi's intricately engineered dialogue has an intimacy that makes seeing *Stereophonic* feel like the luckiest kind of eavesdropping. It throws the audience into the music studio without context, slowly revealing the histories between characters through a charged glance or a moment of easy banter . . . They're making music, but they're destroying each other in the process. The pain is there in the songs—that's what makes them good—but it's immortalized as glory."

—Rebecca Salzhauer, *New Haven Independent*

STEREOPHONIC

OTHER BOOKS BY DAVID ADJMI PUBLISHED BY TCG

1789/1978: Marie Antoinette and 3C

Stunning and Other Plays

ALSO INCLUDES:

Elective Affinities

The Evildoers

STEREOPHONIC

By

DAVID ADJMI

Songs by

WILL BUTLER

THEATRE COMMUNICATIONS GROUP
NEW YORK
2025

Stereophonic is published by Theatre Communications Group, Inc., 520 Eighth Avenue, 20th Floor, Suite 2000, New York, NY 10018-4156

Special thanks to Julie Morris for her generous support of this publication.

TCG books are exclusively distributed to the book trade by Consortium Book Sales and Distribution.

Library of Congress Control Numbers:
2024029427 (paperback) / 2024029428 (ebook)
ISBN 978-1-63670-216-2 (paperback) / ISBN 978-1-63670-217-9 (ebook)
A catalog record for this book is available from the Library of Congress.

Book design and composition by Lisa Govan
Cover photo by Julieta Cervantes, used by permission of SpotCo

First Edition, May 2025

STEREOPHONIC

PRODUCTION HISTORY

Stereophonic had its world premiere at Playwrights Horizons (Adam Greenfield, Artistic Director; Leslie Marcus, Managing Director) in New York City on October 29, 2023. It was directed by Daniel Aukin. The scenic design was by David Zinn, the costume design was by Enver Chakartash, the lighting design was by Jiyoun Chang, the sound design was by Ryan Rumery, the music direction was by Justin Craig; and the production stage manager was Erin Gioia Albrecht. The cast was:

REG	Will Brill
HOLLY	Juliana Canfield
SIMON	Chris Stack
PETER	Tom Pecinka
DIANA	Sarah Pidgeon
GROVER	Eli Gelb
CHARLIE	Andrew R. Butler

The original Broadway production of *Stereophonic* was produced by Sue Wagner, John Johnson, Seaview, Sonia Friedman Productions, Linden Productions, Ashley Melone, and Nick Mills. *Stereophonic* opened at the Shubert Organization's (Robert E. Wankel, Chairman and CEO) John Golden Theatre on April 19, 2024, with the same cast and creative team.

CHARACTERS

REG	British, Bass Player, thirties
HOLLY	British, Lead Vocals, Keyboard, thirties
SIMON	British, Drums, thirties
PETER	U.S., Lead Vocals, Guitar, mid-late twenties
DIANA	U.S., Lead Vocals, Tambourine, mid-late twenties
GROVER	Sound Engineer, late twenties
CHARLIE	Assistant Sound Engineer, mid-late twenties

TIME

The play takes place over the span of a year—1976–1977.

Act I: *A Wizard, A True Star*, June–July 1976

Act II: *Fear of Music*, September 1976

Act III: *Wish You Were Here*, Scene 1, late December 1976; Scenes 2 and 3, March 1977

Act IV: *Goodbye Yellow Brick Road*, June 1977

SETTING

Acts I–III are set in a music studio in Sausalito, CA.
Act IV is set in a music studio in Los Angeles, CA.

AUTHOR'S NOTE

Stereophonic takes place in the control room and sound room of a music studio. The sound room is upstage and completely soundproofed.

I've tried to translate spatial demarcations to the page: dialogue on the left side takes place in the control room; dialogue on the right in the sound room.

This play lives in the space between hypernaturalism and orchestral music. There are lots of carefully choreographed overlaps, sometimes between rooms. A double slash (//) indicates either an overlap or a jump—i.e., no break between the end of one character's speech and the beginning of the following speech. If two sentences abut with no punctuation—or a sentence ends with a question mark followed with a lowercased word—this indicates run-on speech with no break between sentences.

ACT I
A WIZARD, A TRUE STAR

1.

CONTROL ROOM

Simon laying on the sofa, reading Playboy. *It's the Bicentennial Issue.*

SOUND ROOM

Charlie in the sound room going from mic to mic. They're doing the morning "scratch 'n' sniff."

Grover is watching the meters move on the console. Presses the talkback button and speaks into the mic.

GROVER *(talkback)*
Bass drum.

Charlie moves to mic, scratches.

GROVER *(talkback)*
Snare drum.

Charlie moves to mic, scratches.

GROVER *(talkback)*
Got that. You want to go to the toms?

Diana enters the studio, puts down her coat, bag. She bends and gives Simon a tiny side kiss.

Charlie moves to mic, etc. Diana walks through the sound room into the control room.

GROVER *(talkback)*
Great—go to the // Overhead.

SIMON *(quietly sings "Magic Man") "Try to understand . . . try to understand . . ."*

Charlie scratches.

Diana comes back and plops next to Simon.

GROVER *(talkback)*
Okay, now the // bass D.I.

DIANA *(to Simon)*
Why is there no coffee?

SIMON
The coffee machine's broken.

DIANA *(heartbroken)*
What? Oh // come on

SIMON
They're getting // a new one

DIANA
How can it be broken?
we just got here.

He nudges a bag of coke her way.

Charlie scratches.

DIANA
That's not the same // thing

GROVER *(talkback)*
Guitar // D.I.

SIMON
Take it.

DIANA *(cranky)*
No //

SIMON
It's the exact same thing.

Diana relents; cuts two lines of coke. She snorts. One nostril, then the other.

Charlie scratches.

GROVER *(talkback)*
Great can you go to guitar?

Diana twists the bag shut and hands it back to Simon who is sipping from a to-go cup.

DIANA
Where'd you get that?

SIMON
The coffee shop.

He smiles a cheeky smile.

DIANA
What *coffee* shop? Did // you

SIMON
Down*town*.

Charlie scratches.

GROVER *(talkback)*
Piano // left?

DIANA
Where?

SIMON
Right on that main street.

DIANA
What main street?

SIMON
Right in Sausalito, right on
that main street;
there's a coffee shop—it's right
across from Juanita's.

Charlie scratches.

GROVER *(talkback)*
Piano // Right

DIANA
Speaking of Juanita's, where
did you guys go last night?

SIMON
We were looking for you.

DIANA
You were looking for *me*?
I was bored out of my *mind*,
I was // watching television *Charlie scratches.*

Grover gives the thumbs-up.

GROVER *(talkback)*
Can you // go back to the
guitar and play a little?

SIMON
Why didn't you come out
to Juanita's?

DIANA
I *went* to Juanita's // That's
what I'm

SIMON *(sets down the magazine)*
We were there.

DIANA
No one was there //

SIMON
What time did you go?

DIANA
Huh? //

SIMON
What // *time* did

DIANA
I went the time I always go!

SIMON
There is no "always," we've
only been here three days //

Charlie strums the guitar.

DIANA
I went to Juanita's, I was looking
for you guys
and no one was there
and then I went home
and ate a // Swanson's

SIMON *(laughing from the absurdity)*
We were // *there*

DIANA
dinner all by myself //

CHARLIE
Is it clipping? //

SIMON
Are you completely *out // to
lunch*? We were *at Juanita's.*

GROVER *(talkback)*
You're good.

DIANA *(laughing at herself)*
Well I was bored // stiff
Why didn't you just call me?

GROVER *(talkback)*
Holly vocal.

SIMON *(cheeky)*
I was having a good time—am I not allowed to have a good // time?

DIANA
No, you can't have a good time because I want to have a good time too.

Simon makes a "yikes" face, goes back to his magazine. Diana laughs, smacks him playfully on the shoulder. She pulls out her crocheting.

Charlie scratches.

GROVER *(talkback)*
Can you check to see if the mic pre is on?

CHARLIE
Okay //

DIANA *(to herself)*
My head is like a brick.

CHARLIE *(he checks the mic pre)*
It's on.

GROVER *(talkback)*
It's // on?

SIMON
Go have some aspirin.

DIANA
I don't need aspirin I need to get like one hour of sleep. This is // insane

CHARLIE
Is the phantom // power on?

SIMON
I know // I know

Grover checks the phantom power.

DIANA
Did you sleep // through that?

GROVER *(talkback)*
Is the cable // not seated properly?

SIMON
Look at my eyes.

Charlie checks the cable.

DIANA
Oh they're bloodshot.
Oh wait you have something in // your

SIMON
What?

DIANA
C'mere.

Diana picks something out of his eye.

CHARLIE
No, it's not.

DIANA
Okay good. *(instantly cozy) Hiiii.*

SIMON *(instantly charmed)*
Hiiii.

Charlie connects the cable.

DIANA
But you better talk to him and I'm not kidding 'cause I can't talk to // him.

Charlie scratches the mic.

SIMON
Why does everything fall on me?

GROVER *(talkback)*
It's // still not working

DIANA
Because you wanted to be the manager // so

CHARLIE
Let me swap it out.

DIANA
now you // have to manage things, it's

He swaps it out.

GROVER *(talkback)*
Cool //

DIANA
your job to make things go smoothly: *is this smooth*?

SIMON *(faux-naïf)*
Smooth as in?

DIANA
As in people not breaking dishes all night!

SIMON
There are some he didn't // break

DIANA
You do realize—*oh some he didn't break*? uh-huh well we have to pay for all that Simon—it's not our house remember? And Babaloo has to clean up all that glass // Not to mention my

SIMON
So he'll clean the // fucking glass

DIANA
boyfriend is a hypochondriac and now he's constantly gonna think he has glass in his foot //

SIMON
Look: the last album took three weeks, so this can't take more than another two, three weeks *tops*. We can make it two more weeks.

DIANA
Peter said last night he was ready to snap and he wanted to confront Reg and I said no, don't escalate things.

SIMON
It was good you did that.

DIANA *(pointedly)*
And now you have to do your part.

Holly enters and hangs up her jacket. Diana starts to crochet.

CHARLIE
Please mute that channel //

Grover checks the phantom power.

GROVER *(talkback)*
Yep

Holly makes a beeline toward Simon and Diana.

Charlie scratches.

The meters move on the console.

GROVER *(talkback)*
That fixed it.

Charlie gives the thumbs-up.

DIANA
Well anyway I just need my
beauty sleep
that's— *(to Holly)* Hi sweetie
(side kiss) —that's
all // I'm saying

Holly collapses exhausted on the sofa next to Simon, gives him a side kiss.

GROVER *(talkback)*
Let's go to Diana vocal.

Charlie scratches.

Holly sits back up with alacrity, then approaches Grover.

GROVER *(talkback)*
Peter vocal.

Charlie scratches.

HOLLY *(to Grover)*
Oh Grover—

Grover immediately signals for her to wait.

GROVER *(talkback)*
Simon vocal.

Charlie scratches.

GROVER *(talkback)*
Reg vocal.

Charlie scratches.
Charlie gives him a thumbs-up.

GROVER *(talkback)*
Okay we're done.
(to Holly)
Sorry.

HOLLY
No no—sorry I just //

GROVER
No no no—

Charlie enters the control room, sits at the console.

HOLLY
What?

GROVER
What? I // just

HOLLY *(rushing though this)*
Can I just ask you something really quick?

GROVER
Yeah.

HOLLY
Okay, so remember yesterday in the bridge?

GROVER
You mean // the

HOLLY
"*We*"—dah dah dah //

GROVER
Yeah yeah //

HOLLY
Right. So Peter always comes in early
on the "We" // so

GROVER
Right.

DIANA *(to herself)*
We need // a dry cleaner's

HOLLY
So I wanted to add something
Just to hold for a beat so—dah-DAH—
And then hold // And

CHARLIE *(sings)*
"*Dirt in your face*"

GROVER *(as he lights a cigarette)*
Oh right right
Okay yeah I think that's good.

HOLLY
Otherwise—

GROVER
It's // good

HOLLY
Can I steal one?

GROVER
Huh? Oh—yeah //

He gives her a cigarette.

HOLLY
"*We*"— *(hums chords)* and then I come in
with my thing, so it's *(hums chords)*
What do you think? We can try it.

GROVER *(he lights her cigarette)*
Yeah // try it

HOLLY
I think I'll try it.

Holly hums three notes.

DIANA
There's no dry cleaner's in this
part // of town

HOLLY
Yeah okay //

CHARLIE *(sings)*
"Human // race
Dirt in your face"

Holly walks back to the sofa.
Grover sits back down, writes something down.
Holly snuggles next to Simon, eyes shut.

SIMON
What are you talking about Of course
there's a dry cleaner's.

DIANA
Well do you know of a dry cleaner's 'cause
I can't find anything. I look in the phone book
and there's nothing—
the closest one is in Oakland.

SIMON *(duh)*
But Oakland's just across the way //

Grover takes a drag on his cigarette.

DIANA
Oh, it is? Well how do we get there?

SIMON
How do we *get* there? Look on a map.

DIANA
I'm not looking on a map. I have other things to
do with my life if you haven't noticed.

SIMON
Alright // Jesus

DIANA
Holly that place you told me to go,
it does *not* // exist

CHARLIE *(to Grover)*
The room has a really nice decay.

HOLLY *(eyes closed, totally confused)*
What // place?

GROVER *(to Charlie)*
Yeah.

DIANA
The dry cleaner. I was going around in circles.
Will you just go with me?

HOLLY
I gave you the directions.

DIANA
Can you just show it to me?

HOLLY
Yes, I'll show it to you.

Grover produces a cassette, puts it in the player, puts on a pair of headphones.

Grover listens to music while smoking his cigarette.

Simon flips a page in the magazine.

Grover takes a big drag of his cigarette, thinks for a moment.

GROVER *(singing Todd Rundgren's "Is It My Name?")*
"Why don't you love me, dah dah dah dah dah dah
Why don't you love me, bah dah bah bah dah bah"

Grover rocks out to nothing for a moment.
He takes another drag, exhales.

GROVER
"Bah dah bah bah dah bah"

Diana clears her throat and bangs
on her chest.

DIANA
Uch. I need to steam more.

HOLLY
You better watch out because
your voice—

DIANA
I know, I gotta steam.

HOLLY
I can already hear it.

DIANA
It started last year on tour, I was
blowing out my voice on "Dark Night" //

HOLLY
I *told you* //

DIANA
I *know*
Well it's a learning curve, I've never done these
big stadiums // before

SIMON *(turns suddenly to Holly)*
You know who called the house?

HOLLY
It's very taxing on the voice.

SIMON
Holly:

HOLLY
What?

SIMON
Sally MacLeish.

HOLLY
What about her?

SIMON
She called the house.

Holly gives him a look.

HOLLY
How did she get // the number

SIMON
Holly you've *got* to pay her back.

HOLLY
Why is // she always calling me?

SIMON
No listen to me you've got to pay her back She is furious //

HOLLY
I //

SIMON
No I'm not kidding // I'm not kidding—
Listen
Holly I'm being perfectly

HOLLY
Simon.
Simon—

SIMON
serious with you, you have to pay her back, you can't welch.

HOLLY
When did she call?

SIMON
I'm being perfectly serious // with you

HOLLY *(laughing)*
Are we really going to talk about this // right now

SIMON
Alright forget it.

HOLLY
Is she here?

SIMON
Who?

HOLLY
Sally MacLeish

SIMON
No she's // not here She's in Sedona.

DIANA
Who is Sally MacLeish?

HOLLY
What is she doing in bloody Sedona?

SIMON
She's got that *boyfriend* and // she

DIANA *(as she crochets)*
I think // everyone should have a phone in
their room. If we're gonna be living in the

HOLLY
Oh right-right-right-right.

DIANA *(fixes a stitch)*
same house, everyone should have their own line,
I // don't think we should have one hall
phone because everyone's gonna be on
the phone We need to get our messages.

HOLLY *(to Simon)*
Can you call her for me?

SIMON
I don't // want any part of this

HOLLY
I can mail her a check.

SIMON
I don't care if you mail anyone a check I'm just
telling you what Sally MacLeish // told me

HOLLY
I'm not mailing her a check!

SIMON
Don't mail her a check! I don't wanna be in the middle of it.

GROVER *(sings Todd Rundgren)*
"*Bah dah bah bah // dah bah*"

HOLLY
I need coffee.

DIANA
Well the coffee machine's broken.

HOLLY
Again?

DIANA
And he's bringing in this coffee!
He knows the coffee machine
is broken and he won't bring us coffee!

HOLLY
Well give us some of your coffee.

DIANA
How selfish // is that?

HOLLY
Don't be selfish.

SIMON
I'm not selfish. I'm responsible.
I know my needs // and I'm attending to them

DIANA
Well what about my needs What about
Holly's needs Are our needs not
important? // We don't have needs?

SIMON
Your needs are of paramount importance.

DIANA
Well I wish you'd act like it.

He playfully smacks her with the magazine,
Diana grabs it. Simultaneously,
Holly stands abruptly, exits through
the sound room into the kitchen.
Diana looks at the cover, winces.

DIANA
Don't bring this in here!
This is so male chauvinistic My
brother used to have these.

SIMON *(grabs his magazine back)*
Oh I forgot to tell you! Your
song is back in the Top 40.

Diana stops crocheting.

DIANA
My song?

SIMON
Yeah.

DIANA
From the first album?

SIMON
Uh-huh.

DIANA
Is back in the Top 40.

SIMON
Yeah.

She sets down her crochet needles.

DIANA
The single we released a year ago?

SIMON
The very one.

DIANA
That's back in the Top 40?

SIMON
Yeah. It left and then it came back.

DIANA
That's so strange.

SIMON
It's in next week's *Billboard*.

DIANA
Is that normal? For a song to come back into the Top 40?

SIMON
It happens.

DIANA
That's so weird.

SIMON *(loud whisper)*
Bring another song in.

DIANA
Uch, I will.

SIMON
When?

DIANA
Simon, we've been here three days.
Give a girl a minute.

SIMON
Bring something in!

DIANA
I'm shy.

SIMON
I don't think you're shy
I think it's a confidence problem.

DIANA
I do not have a confidence problem
I'm just getting my motors running.

Diana walks over to an open box of donuts.
Peter enters the control room, walks over to Diana.

With Peter's entrance, the energy shifts in the room.
Grover takes off his headphones, Charlie sits up,
the two of them get busy at the console.

Peter spins Diana around, pulls her to him by the waist. He plants a kiss on her, clasps his hands around her.

PETER
Hi sexy lady.

DIANA
Listen I left your // pants,
those two pair of pants—

SIMON *(under his breath)*
"Get your motors running" //

PETER
Yeah where are my pants?

DIANA
Well I was just gonna tell you—
I washed them and
hung them up in the closet.

PETER
You put fabric softener?

DIANA
I put fabric softener.

PETER
Why are you being so nice to me?

DIANA
Because if I'm nice to you
maybe you'll be nice to me.

PETER
So there's a strategy.

DIANA
Every girl needs a strategy.

PETER
I'm so fucking exhausted.

DIANA
Simon's gonna talk to him.

PETER *(checks his watch)*
Do we even know if he's gonna show up?

DIANA
I mean . . . I hope.

They've been unconsciously swaying back and forth the whole time. Diana throws her head back.

DIANA
Wait, I'm getting dizzy.

They stop swaying. Peter grabs his guitar and plays a little riff.

Simon stares at himself in a mirror. He makes an overbite.

DIANA
Hey did you listen to the cassette I left you?

PETER
I will tonight.

DIANA
Okay. 'Cause I just want to know
what you think.

PETER
Why don't you bring it into the room?

DIANA
No no, just listen to it first.

PETER
Okay.

He gives her a peck on the lips.
Simon makes a crazy face in the mirror.
Holly reenters the control room
with a cut up pear.
Peter sees her.

PETER
Pssst!

HOLLY *(rolls her eyes)*
Oh god, please don't start
with // that again

PETER
Ooooh what's *that*?
What is that?

HOLLY
What?

PETER
I want // some

HOLLY
I cut up a pear, what.

Peter grabs a slice of pear.

HOLLY
No no no—that's my pear.
Go get one—

She grabs it back.

HOLLY
Get one in the kitchen.

She gives him a peck on the lips.
Peter checks his watch.

Simon sticks his stomach out in a mirror and pretends to be pregnant.

Peter approaches Grover, puts his arm around him.

GROVER *(to Peter)*
Oh hey man.

PETER
Can we start?

GROVER
I'm ready.

Simon sucks his stomach all the way in, looks at himself in profile.

PETER
Where's Reg?

GROVER
I didn't see him.

PETER
I don't wanna have a bad scene,
but this is the first week.

GROVER
I'm sorry // Peter

PETER
Can you just try to stay on top of it?

GROVER
You want me to call the house?

PETER
You could call the house.

Peter walks off.

GROVER *(to Charlie)*
Call the house.

As Charlie reaches for the phone,
Reg stumbles in. Dead drunk.
Walks an unsteady line to the other
end of the room toward
Diana and Holly.

REG
'Ello mates.

Beat.

SIMON
'Ello mate.

Peter does the riff.

Reg gets very close to Diana and Holly. He reeks of alcohol. It's uncomfortable for everyone.

REG *(slurring)*
What's the scuttlebutt?
What's everyone talkin' about?
(after a pause, to Holly)
Hello darling.

Holly's face becomes a mask. Her eyes shut; it's as though the room has filled with some poisonous gas. She rises; walks into the sound room.

Holly goes to sit at her keyboard.

PETER *(to Grover)*
Can we get him a black coffee?

DIANA
The coffee machine's broken.

SIMON
Grover, where's the bag?

GROVER *(to Charlie, quiet)*
Get the bag.

She plays three quick chords.

CHARLIE
Okay.

They produce the bag of cocaine. Reg prepares a line. Peter suddenly gets a fillip of manic energy, starts jumping up and down.

HOLLY *(sings)*
"We"

PETER
I WANNA PLAY MUSIC!

As Peter makes his way into the sound room, Simon smacks him on the butt repeatedly—which cracks him up.

Holly plays three quick chords. She lights a cigarette.

Simon and Diana make their way to the cocaine bag.

Peter bounds into the sound room.

REG
There was so much fog Simon.
Did you see the fog?
Rolling
Rolling
It's like the moors in England.
Bloody Sausalito.

Peter sits down on a stool and plays a crazy guitar riff.

Reg does a line, gets all coked up. Starts dancing in place.

Holly takes a drag of her cigarette, walks to Peter.

DIANA *(preparing a line of coke)*
You guys Can you
Tell that girl
What's her name—Sally?

GROVER
The receptionist? You mean
Paula?

DIANA
Yeah will you tell her to—
Tell Paula—
I don't // know

She snorts a line.

HOLLY
I was talking to Grover about
that // bridge part

SIMON
Yeah get us a bloody coffee
machine // that works

HOLLY
Cos I was thinking that on the
We // when it goes "We—"

GROVER
I'll tell her //

HOLLY
Dah // dah dah—

SIMON
We get very // tired Grover

PETER
I'm sorry—I keep coming in
early there //

REG
And cold //

HOLLY
Oh it's // fine I was—

SIMON
And Reg // gets cold

HOLLY
I was just thinking
Just to hold for a
second // so—

DIANA
It's just //

HOLLY
dah-DAH—and // then hold

DIANA
It's really hard when you're
here sixteen
hours a day with you // know

PETER
Right.

GROVER
I mean—I'll tell // her

Simon does a bump.

PETER
Or I could just do it the right
way. *(laughs)* I don't know why
I keep coming in early there //

SIMON *(screams)*
Whooo!

He starts jumping up and down and smiling, gliding back and forth.

SIMON *(quoting Monty Python)*
"I will not have my fwends
widiculed by the common
sowldery."

Simon grabs Reg's face.

REG
"I fart in your general direction!"

SIMON
"Your mother was a hamster . . ."

REG AND SIMON
". . . and your father smelt of
elderberries!"

Simon pushes away from Reg
and glides into the sound room
with Reg and Diana following.
Grover waits until they're
all out of earshot.

GROVER *(to Charlie)*
You have to anticipate problems
before they happen.

Charlie's a little confused.

CHARLIE
Okay sorry.

GROVER
You know the four rules of
engineering?

CHARLIE
Um.
No.

GROVER
You need to show up;
You need to *pay attention*;
You need to tell the truth;
And you need to deal
with the consequences Right?

Holly plays a few quick chords.

Peter starts in with guitar.

CHARLIE
Yeah man okay.

Simon slides over to the drums and starts playing a riff.

They're all starting to riff. Diana starts singing the lyrics. Her singing trails off.

PETER
Alright guys let's take it from the top of the second verse.

Simon counts it off with his drumsticks and—

2.

They're all huddled near the console.
Reg has a little blanket wrapped around him.
Diana is draped over Peter.
Peter produces a cassette and hands it to Charlie.

PETER *(to Charlie)*
Can you put this in the tape player?

GROVER
It's new?

PETER
Yeah
It's new.

SIMON
Is this // the

PETER
Yeah this is—remember
Remember I played it on tour
for you? That // little

SIMON
Oh good.

PETER
Yeah let's see.

The tape plays.
We hear Peter singing partial lyrics to guitar—
supplementing his vocals with "da da da," etc.
When the tape finishes they all sit there
for a moment absorbing it.

PETER
Okay so that's the song.
Play that twice,
then solo, chorus I don't know we'll
figure the rest out.

Peter thinks.

SIMON *(to Charlie)*
Can we just hear it again?

Charlie rewinds the tape and presses play,
landing somewhere in the middle of the song.
They listen some more.

HOLLY *(a few seconds in)*
Is this the bridge or the chorus?

Beat.

PETER
Well I thought it was the chorus.

HOLLY
It feels a little like a bridge.

PETER
Yeah you're right.

Peter presses stop on the tape recorder.

SIMON
Yeah She is right.

PETER
What if it's something like . . .

Peter noodles on the guitar.

HOLLY
What if we took that thing from the song
you brought in—you know, the
one we all thought we liked
but we really in the end all hated?

PETER
Which one?

She hums some notes.
Peter plays along to her humming.

PETER
Right.
So how would we do it?
Something like:

He plays, sings, feels it out.
He invents some lyrics on the spot.

PETER
I think it's really good.

HOLLY *(laughing)*
Oh, you like it? I thought you hated it.

PETER
No no no I really like it.

HOLLY
It could be a chorus.

PETER
What if we go . . .

Plays a few notes.

REG
Let's just try it.

PETER
But lemme play it on the electric
Because I don't want it to leak.

REG
Yeah okay.

PETER
Let's move it into the studio.

SIMON
Be right back.

Simon exits. Peter takes off one shoe and examines the bottom of his foot. Diana clocks this—then pretends she hadn't and tries to escape, but Peter sees her.

Blanket-swaddled Reg makes his way into the sound room.

PETER
Can you come here for a second?

DIANA *(deflated)*
Honey, please. I told you,
you don't have glass
in your foot.

PETER
But can you look again?

DIANA *(gingerly)*
Can we look later tonight?

Peter sighs, reluctantly puts his sock and shoe back on.
Holly is about to go in but Diana stops her and whispers something to her.

Grover approaches Peter.

GROVER
I think it's amazing.

PETER
Okay.

Holly and Diana whisper back and forth for a second.

GROVER *(very sincere)*
No really
I have a tremendous respect
for you
I just wanted to say that.

Holly and Diana clasp hands and giggle quietly.

Diana makes her way into sound room.

PETER *(nonplussed)*
Okay.

Grover winces.

Holly is now staring at Grover with the intensity of a laser beam. Grover notices her staring and looks around to see the subject of this Very Intense Gaze. Oh—it's him!

HOLLY *(flirtatious)*
Grover . . . are those trousers
very tight?

GROVER *(disoriented)*
What?

Grover looks down at his pants—are they the wrong size? Holly stands, sashays toward him. When Grover looks back up, she is RIGHT IN HIS FACE.

GROVER *(flinching)*
Oh // *hi*!

HOLLY
Grover
what's that?

GROVER
Huh?

Holly gets uncomfortably close to his face. A discombobulated Grover leans back.

GROVER *(to himself)*
What's happening??

She pulls an eyelash off his cheek, blows it off her index finger.

Reg absently plays a bass riff.

HOLLY
It's good luck.

Holly smiles flirtatiously, blows Grover a little kiss, waves a little wave, then sashays into the sound room. Grover clocks Charlie ogling, then glares back at him: leave it alone.

Holly's sashay is disrupted by the recognition that she's alone in the sound room with Reg. He stops playing bass. She sits augustly at her keyboard and waits. It's horribly tense.

Diana goes back to the control room to get her tambourine.

PETER
Oh we don't need that //

DIANA
What do you mean we don't need it.

PETER
We don't need the tambourine.

DIANA
Really?
(she shakes the tambourine a little)
Okay.

PETER
You okay?

DIANA
So then what am I doing?

PETER
You're singing.

DIANA
I know but like what am I doing with my hands?

PETER
Your *hands*?

DIANA
I mean on tour

I need something to do with
my hands
I can't just stand there.

PETER
Why are you talking about the tour?
I just brought the // song in

DIANA
Yeah but you don't know what
it's like to not have an instrument
and just be standing around
in a huge stadium // while

PETER
Well can't you do this?
(he quickly does a thing)
Something like—you know.
You're always doing these
things with your hands.

Beat.

DIANA *(nonplussed)*
Okay.

Peter limps slightly back into the sound room. Diana follows.

Charlie turns down the volume in the sound room slightly.

Simon enters through the sound room, does a crazy little dance, makes a karate-type move and a noise. He starts doing karate kicks, inching closer to Holly who makes a face. He sits at his drum kit; they begin to rehearse.

CHARLIE
She likes you.

GROVER
Huh?

CHARLIE
Holly.

GROVER
I'm not dipping my chocolate in that
peanut butter.

CHARLIE
She's sexy.

GROVER
She's married
I don't do married.

CHARLIE
So *are* they married or is // she

GROVER *(turns down the volume a bit)*
I don't want to gossip I told you
I don't want any trouble.
They try to rope you in but you gotta
snip the rope,
gotta keep it professional
gotta stay focused, I'm telling you man.

Pause.

CHARLIE
Remember I was telling you about my
buddy Mark?

GROVER
The guy from // the

CHARLIE
Yeah him Mark
my friend from Capital Records;
So he was working on this album down in
Nashville with a country singer,
some chick with pigtails and—
anyway she dressed bad
She was crazy
Freckles and gingham and shit like that ugh.
And wore boots But
like
disgusting plastic crap
Like her boots took a crap on her whole life
She was freaked out on all kinds of
shit ANYWAY.
(he takes a breath)
They balled for like two months
Every night
Every night
She was a sex maniac
And a maniac in general This was in Nashville
And anyway
so he woke up in the middle of the night
one night And she had a piece of glass on
his balls She'd broke a bottle like some feral
awful depressive street bitch.

GROVER *(mutes the volume in the sound room)*
Yeah.

CHARLIE
And she was holding it
on his balls man.

GROVER
Oh shit.

CHARLIE
And she was all you're screwing
another chick
you're screwing a chick
He was all no I ain't she was all
you're screwing around you ARE blah
blah blah So *then*
she cut
like
the bottom of his balls Like
not the *actual* ball?
But the scrotum part and
he was like HEY.
And he took the glass shard from her and
his ball fell onto the mattress
It was like *bloop*;
It was hanging from a string.

GROVER
What string?

CHARLIE
There's a string
And he got stitches and
he's fine now But he
can't play basketball I fucken hate
basketball But he pressed charges
and she cracked up She's in
a mental hospital.
Yeah man.
(beat)
But country singers are all like that.

Johnny Cash?
Merle Haggard?
They're twisted up inside with
that country shit.

Grover sips his beer, lights a cigarette.
Turns up the volume in the sound room.
Smokes for a little bit.
Then very impulsively mutes the sound again
in the sound room, turns to Charlie.

GROVER
Paula is smokin' though.

CHARLIE
The receptionist?

GROVER
She is smokin' hot. I am so
hot for that chick.
I think she wants me.

CHARLIE
Oh yeah man?

GROVER
I mean I think so
It's pretty obvious.

CHARLIE
You could totally see her nipples
in that shirt.

GROVER
Oh I know
She gave me a boner with that shirt.

CHARLIE
I totally also got a boner
Everyone's getting a boner
She's so attractive.
I just want to pour baby oil on her?
And like smear it on her.

Grover laughs.

GROVER
I could totally see her with baby oil
like getting a suntan on a Corvette //

CHARLIE
Oh yeah
and like huge sunglasses.

They high-five.

CHARLIE
You think you can get her to fix
the coffee machine?

GROVER
I feel like she's not super good at her job.
Sometimes when we're talking
the phone just rings and rings
and I'm like fine don't answer it.

Beat.

CHARLIE
So what were you working on before this?

GROVER
Before this album?

CHARLIE
Simon said you were doing something with
The Eagles?

GROVER
Yeah *One of These Nights*

CHARLIE
Oh wow
Do you know Glyn Johns?

GROVER
Yeah I know him //

CHARLIE
And Bill Szymczyk?

GROVER
What about you?

CHARLIE
Huh?

GROVER
What were // you

CHARLIE
Oh
I was working with the Doobie Brothers.

GROVER
Oh yeah?
How'd you get that gig?

CHARLIE
I'm cousins with Tom Johnston.

GROVER *(double take)*
No way.

CHARLIE
Yeah man.

GROVER
Cousins?

CHARLIE
Yeah.

GROVER
You're cousins with the main
Doobie Brother?

CHARLIE
Yeah.

GROVER
You're a Doobie Cousin?

CHARLIE *(laughing)*
We grew up together, yeah.

Grover takes a sip of beer.

GROVER
God man you're lucky,
no one helped me.

CHARLIE
You want another beer?

GROVER
Nah, I'm okay.

Charlie gets a beer.
Grover smiles a Cheshire Cat
smile. He turns to Charlie.

GROVER
I gotta tell you something
but you can't tell anyone.

CHARLIE
What?

GROVER
Well
I never engineered for The Eagles.

CHARLIE *(gives him a look)*
You lied?

GROVER
A white lie.

CHARLIE
That's not a white lie that's—
that's significant.

GROVER
I *worked* on the album
I assisted
so it's not a lie—or it's a lie by
omission.
(beat)
They didn't ask so I didn't say // anything

CHARLIE
They could just check the liner notes //

GROVER
My name's on the album.

CHARLIE
I don't know man
That's pretty nefarious.

GROVER
Everyone puffs up their résumé
it's normal.
I'm twenty-seven
I know what I'm doing
I've engineered like thirteen albums.

CHARLIE
With who?

GROVER
Believe me.

CHARLIE
Are you lying about thirteen
albums Is that also a lie?

GROVER
And I didn't lie—I said I *worked*
with The Eagles
Which is true I just // didn't

CHARLIE
I don't like liars.

GROVER
Never mind.

Short pause.

CHARLIE
So who *did* you engineer for?

Pause.

GROVER *(embarrassed but hiding it)*
The Sybil Sisters?

Beat.

CHARLIE
Who?

GROVER
They got some radio play.
(beat)
You know Tailspin?

Beat.

CHARLIE
No.

GROVER
Oh
Well
And there's this band in Van Nuys . . . Toto?

Charlie screws up his face.

CHARLIE
Toto?

GROVER *(sheepish)*
They're really good.

CHARLIE
Like *The Wizard of Oz*? *Toto???*

GROVER *(burning with shame)*
If you're gonna be an asshole
forget I said anything
faggot.
I was just being open.
I thought you were an open cool person.

CHARLIE
They're gonna find out.

GROVER
No they won't
We just keep giving them coke and booze
We'll do a good job.
(pause)
Everyone makes shit up, it's Hollywood.

CHARLIE
I just don't like liars man.

GROVER
I don't lie in life, just to get a job.

CHARLIE
Don't get feral.

GROVER
I just need a foot in the door
I don't know anyone
You know?

Beat.

CHARLIE *(softens)*
Yeah.

Grover smiles a bittersweet smile.

GROVER
I don't have a Doobie Cousin.

Grover starts laughing.

Peter is signaling to him from the sound room.

Grover turns the volume back on.

GROVER
What's that, Peter?

PETER
I was asking you if—
What are you doing, man? You need to be paying attention.

GROVER
I'm sorry
The mic was off.

PETER
You need to keep that mic on.
You need to pay attention, Grover.

GROVER
Sorry.

PETER
The guitar sounds too thin in my phones, can you fatten it up?

Grover adjusts on the console.

Peter strums.

PETER
A little more.

Grover adjusts again.

Peter strums.

PETER
Okay better.
Pay: *attention*.
(to the band)
Okay let's give it another churn?

3.

Band members and both engineers clustered around the console.
Holly has a mug of tea, Reg drinks a beer.

SIMON
So I spoke to Rick at the label and I just wanna say two quick things. The first is—and it'll be out in next week's *Billboard*—but "Dark Night" just cracked the Top 10.

DIANA
But we know this already

SIMON
No no—not the top forty, the top *ten*.

Beat.

DIANA *(disbelief)*
My song?

SIMON
It's at number eight.

Diana starts to absorb this piece of information: a complicated swirl of elation, embarrassment, and genuine shock. She anxiously looks to Peter—who looks like he might burst into tears.

PETER *(forcing excitement)*
That's amazing!

He claps. It's a bit awkward.

SIMON
And for whatever reason, a year and a half later, the album is back in the Top 40. I think we're at, like . . . thirty-two? It'll be in next week's *Billboard.*
(beat)
Second thing is, Columbia tripled our budget.

Holly laughs in disbelief and looks around—everyone looks shocked.

HOLLY *(shock)*
Tripled?

Beat.

SIMON
We no longer have to be out by
the end of the month.
We can stay as long as we want.
(beat)
Anyone have a // comment?

HOLLY
But don't we *want* to be out by
the end of the month?

SIMON
Don't look so fucking grim;
this is a *good thing*.

Holly takes a deep breath.

SIMON
Anyone else have a comment?
(no one does)
Okay. Let's take a quick break,
yeah?

A flurry of simultaneous activity:

Charlie and Grover start adjusting levels on the console, organizing track sheets, etc.

Simon quickly whispers something to Reg, who laughs in response. Holly goes over to Diana, grabs her face and sweetly bumps noses with her, as a discreet congratulations. They whisper to one another as Peter watches from

Simon enters the sound room.

the sidelines—smiles, but he's covering. Reg exits into the sound room.

Holly enters the sound room, joins Simon off to the side, where they speak sotto voce. Holly lights a cigarette.

Diana anxiously gazing over at Peter; screws up the courage to go over to him.

Reg enters the sound room, grabs his bass, sits, strums absently. Every so often, Holly notices Reg; shoots him a dirty look.

DIANA
Are you okay?

PETER *(covering)*
Yeah are you crazy?
Of course I'm okay.
(pause)
I'm so happy for you.

DIANA
Really?

PETER
Really.

Beat.

DIANA *(somewhat uncertain)*
Okay

Peter exits.
A somewhat deflated Diana exits the studio through the opposite door.

Once the coast is clear:

GROVER *(to Charlie)*
The budget was already huge
to begin with, they had a huge
budget. I'm kinda freaking out
Are you freaking out?

CHARLIE
No.

GROVER
But this is like the biggest
budget ever for an album;
this is a *huge* // budget

Diana sits and crochets at the back of the room.

CHARLIE
No it's not.

GROVER
Dude, *yes it is*: they're getting
more than Pink Floyd got
for *Dark Side of the Moon* //

HOLLY
Could you be a // love

GROVER
That's a lot of pressure.

SIMON
Always.

HOLLY
Could you please let him know
that I'm changing the chord
in "Drive" to an E minor //

CHARLIE
Wait how do you know that?

GROVER
Know what? //

CHARLIE
About *Dark // Side of the Moon*

Simon hesitates for a moment, sighs.

GROVER
Because I heard Simon talking on the phone I didn't put it all together until just now.
I'm freaking // out

CHARLIE
It's still the same // job

SIMON *(clears his throat, to Reg)*
She's changing the chord to an // E minor

GROVER *(under his breath)*
Holy shit holy shit //

REG
Tell her I'm not changing that.

GROVER
No no // no You're right
You're right. Be cool.

HOLLY
Tell him he's gonna change it because the song's in a different key now.

GROVER
Be cool.

REG
Tell her to change the bloody key back to what it was.

Reg marches into the control room.

REG
Where's the bag.

Charlie hurriedly gets him the bag of cocaine. Reg does two lines. He finds a bottle of Jack Daniel's and takes a huge swig.

Holly and Simon watch him from the sound room.

Reg storms out of the studio. As he leaves, Peter enters with a beer. He cracks it open, takes a swig. He sits at the sofa, thumbs through a magazine.

Upon noticing Peter, Diana puts down the needles. She stands, takes a breath and walks into the control room.

Diana hesitates for a moment, then walks to Peter. Peter looks up from his magazine. She looks like she's just come in from a storm. Brief silence.

DIANA *(tentatively)*
I have something.

PETER
Oh yeah?

DIANA
I just did it last night.

With some anxiety, she pulls a folded piece of paper from her pocket, hands it to him.

Peter unfolds the page, glances at it, then looks up at her.

PETER
When did you write this?

DIANA
Last night.

Peter glances at the page again.

Simon plays the drum riff.

Grover exits.

Charlie puts on a pair of headphones, plays something on the tape player.

PETER
Why didn't you show it to me last night?

DIANA *(anxious)*
You said to bring stuff into the room.

Beat.

PETER
Yeah . . . Yeah . . . No, of course.

DIANA
Is that okay?

PETER *(nervous laugh)*
Stop asking me if I'm okay, I'm fine.

DIANA *(biting her cuticles)*
Can you read my handwriting?

He's transfixed.

PETER
I can read it
Yeah.

DIANA
What.

Peter just shakes his head.
He reads it again, he nods.

PETER
Okay . . .
(he looks right in her eyes)
Okay.
Do you have a riff?

Simon stops playing the drums.

DIANA
I have like . . . the *beginning*
of a riff.

PETER
Okay.

DIANA
So it's sort of—Remember the
thing we were
working on in 1970 in the
summer in your // father's

PETER
Yeah // the

DIANA
Where you had that
long long guitar solo //
and we cut the

PETER
Yep //

DIANA
So it's not that
But it's // sort

PETER
With the
Yeahyeahyeah.

Peter's fingering his guitar, remembering as he's saying it.

DIANA
of like that. Let me
show you.

Diana enters the sound room. Peter follows. She sits at the keyboard. She lifts her hands to play, feels herself being watched.

DIANA
Could you all not look at me?
I'm nervous.

She takes a deep breath.

DIANA
So it's in a minor key
and it's like this:

She starts to play.

DIANA

Sunday morning
And the light is fine
In the beating of a bird's wing
I come alive

I was dreaming
Of a love song
But what good is love
When the wind starts blowing?

Nothing's forgotten
Nothing's forgiven
When the night comes to an end

Like the bird on the windowsill
I tremble
Through the passing shadow
Close my eyes and count to ten
Until

I'm in the bright light
Forgetting my name
The shadow of our lives
Familiar but strange

Without enough darkness left to
Hide all the pain
I'm in the bright light again

And then I don't know the rest
And then there's a bridge
And it goes—and I think it
jumps

It's
We move up a key.

Stunned silence.

SIMON
I love it.

They all look to Peter.

PETER
How many more verses are there?

DIANA
Five?

PETER
It's a little long.

DIANA
I don't think it's long.

PETER
A little bit.

DIANA
Do you think you could do something with it?

PETER
Yeah let's see.

HOLLY
Let's just start working.

Pause.

PETER
Gimme a minute?

He exits. There's an awkward silence. Diana folds her paper and puts it in her pocket. She smiles to cover.

4.

A week later. It's the end of the day.
Simon's rolling a joint in the control room.
Reg, sitting at the console, swaddled in his
usual blanket, watches. He's somewhat glum.
Peter's playing with an Etch A Sketch.

SIMON
I got this *gaaanja.*
(preps the joint)
Gonna have me some fun tonight.
Elke Holland's friend
has a pot farm
You know Elke.

REG
What's she, the blond?

SIMON
Yeah
Swedish bird
You met her at Don Henley's party.
(runs into a joint-rolling problem and fixes it)
Oh yeah
She's a real tart that Elke.
Elke Holland.

Simon wiggles his eyebrows at a nonresponsive Reg.
He shows Reg some of the pot.

SIMON
Look how bright:

REG *(slightly glum)*
Oh yeah
Yeah it's like fluorescent.

Beat.

SIMON
You alright?

REG
Me?

SIMON
Yeah.

REG
I'm just feelin' a little under the weather.
I think I'm getting a cold in the nose.

SIMON *(old hag voice)*
A cold in the nose?

REG

Yeah.

SIMON

You know what's good for a
cold in the nose?
Mari-wuana
Mary-wua-na
(beat)
Mary-mary-mary-*wuana.*
(he hands him the joint)
Wanna?
(wiggles his eyebrows)

PETER

I'M MESSIN' IT UP!

Peter starts shaking the Etch A Sketch
very vigorously, begins a new drawing.

Simon lights the joint, hands it to Reg.
Reg takes a toke, passes to Simon.
They pass the joint back and forth.

REG *(tentative)*

Simon
I been thinking
What if we co-manage the band together
Me an' you.

SIMON

You don't think it'll be too much pressure?

REG *(hurt)*

Why do you say that?

SIMON
I mean . . . you're not exactly your
best self at the moment.

REG
It'll give me something to do.
It'll give me discipline.
I can throw my whole self into
the band That's when I'm happiest.
(beat)
My wife doesn't want to be with me.
Got to find something
to live for.

SIMON
Why do you have to be such a sad man in a
blanket all the bloody time Eh?
Sad, sad man in a blanket.
I'm lonely too, you know.
I haven't seen Elyse since the tour.
I haven't seen my kids in months.
But I can't talk about killing myself all day, can I.

Reg glumly stares back at him.
Simon claps his hands together.

SIMON
Alright, I'll tell you what we're gonna do:
We're gonna finish this joint
we're gonna go back home
I'm gonna cook you up a nice dinner
we'll have a few pints, maybe get a couple of girls—

REG *(wincing)*
No girls.

SIMON
Alright No girls.
It's *your* night.
Whatever *you* want, Reggie.

REG *(slight smile)*
Yeah okay.

Reg takes another toke,
gets lost in thought.

SIMON *(to Peter)*
Where's Diana?

PETER
Home.
(beat)
She's watching some . . . sports thing.

SIMON
Sports thing?

PETER
Yeah, you know
The Olympics?

Simon hands him the joint,
Peter takes a huge
toke, passes it back to Simon.
He lies down on the floor
alongside them. They all take
turns passing the joint.

REG
You know I've been walking around
Taking these long walks.

SIMON
Good for the system, long walks.

REG
Yeah. Yeah long walks
Yeah I went down to Waldo Point,
you been down there?
Met this bloke—Sal—one of the locals.
Sal was telling me about these houseboat wars.

PETER
What's that?

REG
Houseboat Wars—yeah it's really interesting.
(the pot hits him now)
Houseboat wars.
See, there are four hundred
well almost—almost four hundred—or
something.
Or *three* hundred . . .
at least a hundred houseboats.

SIMON
Where?

REG
Five, six hundred meters from downtown?
All these houseboats.
And underneath
there are streets mapped out
platted—under the water
it's all platted out.

SIMON
You don't say.

REG

Yeah. See they wanted to
extend the shoreline
and make it a street
And that led to a whole series of
very contentious
really brutal confrontations actually,
because the houseboat people said
we're living on a street
and we have every right to be here
And the Hill People disagree.

PETER

What the fuck are Hill People?

REG

Hill People
Rich, you know—establishment types.
Yeah.
So the Hill People
declared war on the Houseboat People
It's been going on a long bloody time.
They *burn* the houseboats;
they throw *eggs* at the houseboats;
it's brutal.

SIMON

That is brutal.

They contemplate this brutality briefly.

REG

I think it's interesting.

SIMON

Yeah.

REG *(to Peter)*
Don't you think it's interesting?

PETER
I think it's interesting.

REG
But . . . I mean *really* do you think
it's // interesting

PETER
I just said I think it's interesting.

REG
No but I mean that there could be this
whole alternate way of living
This whole community of people that
found a way to transcend life.
And it's right down the street!
Five hundred meters
Huge
you can't miss 'em They're almost
They're like kinetic sculpture.
It's like Mecca!
It's like the mountain!
It's like mythology!
Like all of these great artists
comin' to these houseboats
It's a calling!
Otis Redding?
He wrote "(Sittin' On) The Dock of the Bay"
on a houseboat.

SIMON
Otis Redding did not live on
a bloody houseboat.

REG
That's the dock! That's the bay!
Sittin' on the dock of the bay!
Sal told me about it!

PETER *(hysterically laughing)*
Who's Sal?

REG
And there's a whole group!
Alan Watts?
Otis Redding?
Shel Silverstein—who is a genius—
they all had *houseboats*
Baby Face Nelson?

PETER *(tickled)*
Who?

REG
Baby Face!
The gangster from the 1920s
You know him
(he does a Cagney impersonation
trying to be intense but it makes them laugh)
"Nyah"
"NYYAAAAAH"
"Why that dirty no good yellow-bellied stool"
Baby Face!! "Nyaaaaaaahhhh."

His mind is momentarily blown.

REG
Sausalito man? It's incredible.
It's *blowing my mind.*

Short pause.

PETER
What's on for tonight // you guys?

REG
The houseboats are like sculptures
and that's what I want.
A kinetic sculpture to live in
on the water.
I want to live in art.

Beat.

PETER
So you making dinner or something?

SIMON
I think I'm gonna cook up a chicken
Tonight
I think so.
(looks at Reg) Would you fancy that?
Chicken on a brick?

REG
A real brick?

SIMON
Yeah.

REG
Why do you cook it?

SIMON
My grandmum taught me mum how to make it.
Chicken smashed by a brick.

REG
Sounds brutal.

They pass the joint around.

PETER
There's a sauce or no sauce?

SIMON
No sauce. Just a brick.

PETER *(coy)*
I'd love to uh join you for dinner I mean
if I'm not bothering anyone.

Uncomfortably long beat.

REG
No. No bother.

PETER
Chicken's my favorite.
I used to eat buckets and
buckets of chicken with my cousin.
We'd go to this chicken place
in downtown Phoenix?
It was pretty famous. Like this kind of legendary
chicken place?
(they pass the joint around)
I haven't seen my cousin in so long.
We were close as kids—we were
really close when we were kids.
I was gonna go to Montreal
to see him // but um

SIMON
Is that where he lives?

PETER
Where?

SIMON
Montreal?

PETER
No, he's at the Olympics.

SIMON
Why is he at the Olympics?

PETER
Oh, my whole family's there.
My brother's competing.

SIMON *(taken aback)*
Your *brother*?

PETER
Yes, he's a swimmer.

SIMON
In *the Olympics*.

PETER
Yes, he's an Olympic champion. I told you that.

SIMON
You never told us that.

REG
I never heard that before.

PETER
That's why Diana's watching the Olympics
She's watching my brother.

SIMON
Well why aren't *you* watching
your brother?

PETER *(smiles)*
Because I'm working, okay?
I'm trying to make a fucking record.
(nervous laugh)
God this pot is so strong
Where'd you get this stuff?

REG
Well, if my brother was in the
Olympics I would watch it.

PETER
He's good, but I think he's a
little overpraised.
And I think
I don't think swimming is actually—and
my father would kill me right now—but
I don't think it's actually a sport.

SIMON
You *don't*.

PETER
I think it's trivial.

REG
Trivial
It's not trivial
It's hard to become a swimmer
to become an Olympic swimmer?

That's very difficult Peter
not everyone can do that
That takes a lot of work and a lot of skill.

Beat.

PETER *(polite)*
Yeah, I'm sure you're right.

Pause.

REG
Sometimes you can be slightly critical.

PETER
I'm not being critical. I'm just saying that swimming is a technique, and you just have to learn the technique, and practice and then anyone can do it.

Reg takes this in.

REG
You're somewhat critical.

PETER
You think I'm critical of *you*?

REG
Like . . . I think . . . well it's not really important.

PETER
No, say it.

REG
Look, Peter: I know we're very different
you know
even the way we play music //

PETER
I'm never critical of you, Reg.
I'm always helping you,
you're my bandmate.
(beat)
I sometimes feel a little misunderstood.

REG
I don't mean to misunderstand you.

PETER
No, you're deliberately
misunderstanding me.

REG
Peter, that's not // true

PETER
You always do this thing
where I'm the *American* and I'm *vain* and
I'm an *asshole* I don't // like it!

REG
I'm not doing that.

PETER
Oh you're not?

REG
No.

PETER
So what do you think you're doing?
In your mind?

REG *(confused)*
In my *mind*?

PETER
Yeah, in your *mind*—what are you doing?
When you put me in this little box? What
are you saying to yourself about me?

REG *(flummoxed)*
I think you're very talented.

PETER
No. No. That's *not* what you say!
But you know what?
You know what?
At least I don't keep people up in the middle
of the night with my coke binges and
my drinking! At least I'm considerate and
clean my dishes!
(he stands, utterly shaken)
This could have been a brotherly night.
We could have had a whole brotherly feeling
for each other and now you've ruined it and I
want that. I *want* that for us—don't you
want that?

SIMON
Peter—

PETER
Don't you want it to be *brotherly*
between us? Don't you want to be more

than just a bunch of strangers playing music together? I want that. I want us to have dinner together! And eat Simon's chicken!

SIMON

You can still have // it

PETER

No, forget it, I'm going to the Italian place.

SIMON

Don't go // to the Italian

REG

Peter //

PETER

I'm *going* to the Italian place
And I'm having a glass of Asti Spumante!
And I'm gonna *eat* ravioli and *calm down*!
'Cause I'm *stoned*!
And *you know* I'm stoned!

As he starts to exit, he notices a slight limp in his left foot.

PETER

And now I have *glass in my foot*!

He limps out.

A brief moment of reflection.

SIMON

I hate to say this, but he does have a point.

REG
Oh *man* . . .

SIMON
Look mate,
if you want to have a pint by all means do.
But you're drinking way too much
And you're taking way too much blow
And you're keeping us all up
It's affecting the band.

REG
I miss Holly.

Simon glares at him.

SIMON
Sad, sad man.

REG
I do.

SIMON
Sad little man in a blanket.

REG
Sod off.

SIMON
Sad little man trudging around
in a wet Indian blanket.
And your nose is cold
And your joints hurt
(Reg hits him) And your little pajamas
are all soiled and soggy

(Reg makes a cranky noise)
Little Daddy Wumpum.
(Simon pokes him)
Wumpum
(Simon pokes him again, Reg jumps)
Wumpum wumpum.
(pokes him a few times, tickling him a little)

REG *(giggling)*
Stop it, stop it.

They're laughing and
poking each other.

REG *(hysterically laughing)*
Stop it! *Stop!*

5.

Morning.

Peter plays on his guitar, mouthing lyrics. He stops for a moment, jots something down on a piece of paper, plays a bit more.

Diana on the couch, smoking a cigarette. She very suddenly gets an idea, pulls a pad out from her pocket and starts writing.

Peter stops playing, walks out of the room.

Pause.

Holly walks in the room, puts her coat down, collapses on the floor. Diana starts laughing.

DIANA *(giddy from exhaustion)*
What are you doing?

HOLLY *(also exhausted)*
Nothing.

DIANA
Why are you on the floor?

No answer.

DIANA
Come here.

HOLLY
No you come here.

DIANA
Come *over* here.

HOLLY
No I'm dead.

DIANA
Come on . . . I'm reaching out.
Reach back!

They reach out to one another
from across the gulf of the room,
but it's ridiculous.
Holly gives up.

HOLLY
Do you have a light?

DIANA
Yeah, come here.

HOLLY *(reluctant)*
Alright.

She gets on all fours and stumbles over.
Diana lights Holly's cigarette.
They're sitting there smoking together.
Holly spots a box of donuts.

HOLLY
Ooh.

DIANA *(playing along)*
Ooh.

HOLLY *(looks over to Diana)*
Ooh!

Diana laughs. Holly hops over to the donuts.

HOLLY
Sugar sugar sugar!

Holly opens the cover to the box.

HOLLY
Ooh! Is this the Holiday assortment?
Do I see a Holiday // assortment before me?

Holly begins dissecting the donuts with
her fingers, one by one.

DIANA
Don't open every donut!
They get stale really quick.
Oh my // god

HOLLY
When I look back
On my deathbed
when I shuffle off this mortal coil
(she holds the donut up to the light like
it's some magnificent crystal)
This is the memory I shall
cherish most dearly
In all my life
for all eternity
this pink plastic cylindrical . . .
(she examines it, half disgusted)
Food
Thing
This . . . this comestible
bit of sheen.

She takes a bite of the donut.

HOLLY
It's so pretty.

DIANA
When I was a little // girl

HOLLY
"Pretty // pretty"

DIANA
When I was // a little girl We had the

HOLLY *(helpless)*
I'm so tired.

DIANA
best donut shop in—It was
on MacDowell Avenue—which
was where all the shops were
And oh my god they did a Boston Cream—

HOLLY
That's the jizzy one.

DIANA
What?

HOLLY
You heard me.

DIANA
It's not
OH // MY GOD.

HOLLY
Yes it is.

DIANA
Now you're ruining my
like
my whole *childhood.*
You don't like *custard*?

HOLLY
I love custard.

DIANA
So?

HOLLY
That's not custard.

DIANA
Yes it is
It's delicious custard.

HOLLY
It is not delicious custard
I've had custard
I can—I *make* custard.

DIANA
How do you *make* it?

HOLLY
You—

DIANA
What is it? It's eggs?

HOLLY
Eggs?

DIANA
Right?

HOLLY
It's not eggs.

DIANA
Well how do you make custard?

HOLLY
It's a powder.

Diana cracks up.

HOLLY
Why are you laughing?
That's British custard anyway
My mum made us crumble with this
powder thing.

Diana's having a laughing fit.

HOLLY
And you had—*honestly*—it was this
powder and you put steamed
milk and—*why are you laughing*?

Diana's laughing convulsively,
tears leaking from her eyes.

DIANA
Because that's not *real*!!

HOLLY
It is!

DIANA
I thought you were gonna tell me
I thought you had some like
ancient British *custard* recipe.

HOLLY
It's real to me.

They smoke for a little, Diana does a line of coke.

Diana shakes her head, starts laughing and
covers her eyes. Holly sits next to her on
the sofa, gives her a little squeeze, kiss on cheek.

HOLLY
Okay. Now:
(she clasps Diana's hands in hers)
I want to tell you something
and I don't want you to get upset.

DIANA
Oh my god, *what*?

HOLLY
Okay, don't freak out . . . but . . .
I'm moving out of the house.

DIANA
What house?
(beat)
Our house?
You're moving out of *our* // house?

HOLLY
No, it's *okay*—it's *okay*! It's *good*;
I bought a condo.

DIANA *(incredulous)*
You bought a *condo*?

HOLLY
In Tiburon—*yeah*, but // it's—

DIANA
Wait-wait-wait back up:
You're leaving the // *house*? *When?*

HOLLY
It's just twenty minutes // away

DIANA
No! You can't leave me there!

HOLLY
You can come over. It's *good*!
We can have our own space!

DIANA
But it's *not* my space.
I can't believe you would abandon me
like this. I can't live with these
disgusting men!

HOLLY
But you understand my position.
You know what it's been like, I can't
take it // anymore

DIANA
You can't leave me with them—*I*
can't take it either, I haven't slept in
like three weeks.

HOLLY
Okay, look: Just come with me.

DIANA
What? *Really?*

HOLLY
Yeah
There's a bunch of empty ones.
You get one, the one next door isn't sold yet.

Simon enters the control room, wearing a turban, doing a Mick Jagger–type strut over to Holly and Diana without them noticing.

DIANA
I can't—
(laughs)
When do you have time to *do* these things?
You bought a *condo*?
We're in here like
sixteen hours a day—when do you have
time to buy real estate?
I'm so confused by you.
(beat)
And aren't we gonna be done in a
week anyway? why are you—

SIMON *(practicing American accent)*
"Whatcha doin'?"
You like that? like my accent?
"Whatcha doin'"

HOLLY
Go get some coffee There's a fresh
pot in the kitchen.

SIMON
"Whatcha whatcha whatcha"

DIANA *(to Holly)*
So where is this condo again? You // said

HOLLY
Tiburon.

SIMON
What condo?

DIANA *(consoling herself)*
Okay . . . not that far.

HOLLY
It's a tree-lined street; it's pretty.

SIMON
You bought a condo in Tiburon?

DIANA
She's moving out of the house.

Beat.

SIMON
Oh.
(pause)
But Tiburon is . . .
I mean it's terrible, right?

HOLLY
But it's far enough from here that
I'll get space,
and it's quiet, there's a garden
bisected by a stone path.

DIANA
That sounds good.

HOLLY
There's a little sort of
cloister area with a statue
And daffodils.

(beat)
I just want a bit of peace.

DIANA
I know you do.

Grover and Charlie walk in with Reg. Reg is wasted. He's carrying a half-empty bottle of scotch.

GROVER
Hey Simon.

SIMON
Holly bought a condo.

A mortified Diana covers her face with her hands.

GROVER
Who bought a condo?

SIMON
This one over here.

Pause.

REG
You're not leaving the house.

HOLLY
Oh yes I am.

REG
I'm not paying for it.

HOLLY
I have my own money.

REG
I don't understand—
why you have To just
To *waste*
All this *money* when we have a fucking place.
(very vulnerable)
I just
I really don't want you to leave.

HOLLY
Let's talk about this in private

REG
IT'S PRIVATE IN FRONT OF THEM!

SIMON
Reg—

REG *(profoundly upset)*
I'VE DONE NOTHING TO YOU
NOTHING
(beat)
YOU WERE THE ONE!
I WAITED UP ALL NIGHT!
YOU LEFT THE HOTEL ROOM
YOU HAD A *STRATEGY*

HOLLY *(discomfited)*
Oh I had a *strategy*? // Oh *okay*, that's it
you have me all figured out

REG *(desperately hurt)*
IN *CLEVELAND*!
IN *CLEVELAND*, YOU SAID YOU WERE
STAYING IN THE HOTEL ROOM!
BUT YOU *DIDN'T* STAY.

Holly makes herself very steely
and very quiet.

HOLLY
I'm not wiping your face anymore in
the middle of the night so you
don't choke on your vomit.
I'm not coming to the pub at four A.M.
to pick you off the floor.
(beat)
I'm not cleaning up your mess
anymore, I won't do it.

A horrible silence.

SIMON
Reg
Come on man.

REG *(tentative)*
Yeah. Sorry.
(his breath is all liquor and
Simon has to wave it off)
Yeah . . . right
yeah.

Simon takes away his liquor.

Diana whispers something to Holly.
Holly nods—she's okay.

Grover produces the bag of coke
and gives some to Reg.
Diana breaks her hug with Holly,
whispers something.

GROVER
That'll wake you up
Alright? Go on.

Reg does a couple of hits.

Simon approaches Holly.
Diana exits into the sound room.

HOLLY *(warning)*
Don't take his side.

SIMON
No one is taking anyone's side
Just keep it out of the room
is all I'm asking.

HOLLY
As long as we're both part of
this band it's going to be in
the room and it's going to be
bloody uncomfortable.

Diana goes to her music stand,
finds a mug of tea, and has a sip.

SIMON
Point // taken—

HOLLY
I can't very well hide
under my keyboard.

SIMON
I know that but he's very fragile
Can you just—
just try to be a little bit
nice here and there.

HOLLY *(livid)*
You be nice.

Reg enters the sound room.

She lights a cigarette,
her hand shaking.

Pause.

CHARLIE *(to Holly)*
My sister got a condo.

Simon walks into the sound room
and sits at his drums.

CHARLIE
She lives in Chicago.
I'm not a condo guy
Personally
I could never live in a condo.
(beat)
I'll come to the
housewarming party
I'm not saying that
I'll visit
You have me over
I'll come over.
I'll take off my shoes
I'm a good guest
I won't dirty your floors.

HOLLY *(bemused)*
Okay.

Peter walks back into the sound
room; he's munching on an apple.
He crunches on his apple again,
swallows.

Diana gives him a look. Grabs her tambourine. Everyone sits at their instruments.
Peter shrugs.

PETER *(grabbing his guitar)*
I wanna play musiiiiccc!

Simon gives Peter a look.
He doesn't notice.
A still furious Holly enters the sound room.
Peter starts playing a riff on the guitar then stops.

PETER
Reg, I have an idea for "Domino."

REG
What's that?

PETER
What about a different bass part? Something a little . . . you know, with less movement?

Simon sighs, frustrated.

REG *(still recovering)*
You said it was too static before.

PETER
I know.

But now it's a little too far the
other way
Let me show you.

Peter takes Reg's bass and plays the riff.

PETER
What do you think?

Beat.

REG
It's different.

PETER
Right?

REG
It's definitely different. Let's add some more instruments and see.

Peter quickly plays the riff once more.

REG
I have to hear it a few more times. It's hard to get used to this. It's not right to me but—
(beat)
Can you make a cassette of the track so I can have a listen at home? I need to get used to it.

PETER
Yeah. Definitely.

REG
To know more of . . . what you want.

PETER
Don't make it too dressed up—just play it straight. Keep it really simple, okay? Don't make it too—don't put all that stuff in.

Simon gets on the drums and starts to groove.

PETER
Roots and fifths.
Roots and fifths.

Peter starts to play along to Simon's riff, which is a signal for the rest of the band to resume rehearsal—they all get in place.

Holly plays a few chords.

PETER
Okay, guys—I think we're in good shape with "Drive." Should we put one down? Holly, what do you think, should we put one down?

HOLLY *(after disoriented beat)*
What?

Beat.

PETER
You okay?

HOLLY *(sinister)*
Don't I look okay?

PETER *(a little taken aback)*
Well—you—

HOLLY *(with sublimated rage)*
Let's just record!

GROVER *(talkback)*
Let's put one down.
(to Charlie)
Roll tape
(Charlie rolls tape;
talkback)
We're rolling.
"Drive"
Take one.

Meters moving.
Red lights on the console.
Tape moving.

Simon counts off with his
drumsticks. They start playing.

HOLLY
Whatever wakes you in the
morning

Whatever keeps you up at night
Whatever diamonds you've been hiding
Afraid they'll cheapen in the light
Outside, winter winds are blowing

DIANA AND PETER
Ooh oooooh

HOLLY
And the stars are trying to shine

DIANA AND PETER
Ooh oooooh

HOLLY
In a car you can't afford
We just drive and drive and drive
I feel it once again

DIANA AND PETER
I feel it once again

HOLLY
Love waiting in the wind

DIANA AND PETER
Love waiting in the wind

HOLLY AND DIANA
Beyond the next horizon
We've got to keep on driving

HOLLY
We move—

Holly interrupts.

HOLLY *(more sublimated rage)*
Peter
You came in early again.

Charlie stops the tape machine.

PETER
I did?

HOLLY
I already changed it for you
and you came in a measure
early again
I said *hold* and then "dah—
DAH" And then *hold*.

PETER
Right.

HOLLY
And *then* you come in "BAH
BAH"

PETER *(meek)*
I'm so sorry.

HOLLY *(terse)*
Yeah.

PETER
I wasn't sure if we were doing
the hold thing or not.

Holly shuts her eyes for a moment.

GROVER
Let's give it another go.

SIMON
Wait wait
Grover give us a minute.

Simon loosens the snares.

GROVER
Can we fix the EQ on the snare?
Take it up 10K.
Brighten it up a little yeah?

Charlie does it.

HOLLY
Can I get a bit more reverb?

PETER
And can we get more bass on the cans?

HOLLY
Can I get more bass as well?

REG
I'd like more bass // as well

PETER
Give everyone more bass.

Grover fixes the levels on their headphones.

HOLLY
I'm getting too much of
Simon's drum;
I need more of me
And I can't hear Peter.

Grover fixes the levels.

GROVER
Okay like
can you guys all play a little bit?

Holly's listening on her headphones.

HOLLY
I still can't hear Peter.

Grover fixes something.

HOLLY
Now I hear too much of Peter
All I hear is guitar.

Grover fixes it.

HOLLY
Okay.

GROVER
Everyone good?

SIMON
Yep.

GROVER
Ready to lay it down?

SIMON
Let's do it.

GROVER *(talkback)*
Okay stand by.
(to Charlie)
Roll tape.
(Charlie rolls tape; talkback)
We're rolling. "Drive," take two.

They start to play.

HOLLY
Whatever wakes you in the morning
Whatever keeps you up at night

Peter stops them.

Charlie stops the tape.

PETER
Sorry—
It feels rushed to me.

SIMON
What do you mean?

PETER
There's no space.

SIMON
Why does it feel rushed to you?
I think it feels okay.

HOLLY
How does it sound Grover?

GROVER
Why don't you come in and have a listen?

HOLLY *(cold)*
No I don't want to "have a listen." I don't have time to come in there and "have a listen" every bloody time we lay something down.
(beat)
What are you doing out there?
Why can't you be listening to us and paying attention to what's going on *in here*?
(tense pause)
You start paying attention to

the tempo *and* the key *and* the instruments and give us a little *fucking help*.

GROVER *(talkback)*
I'm not producing this album.

HOLLY
I don't bloody care!
I don't care if you're bloody producing the BLOODY ALBUM
It's still *YOUR JOB*!

GROVER *(talkback)*
Okay. I'll start being more vigilant.

SIMON *(trying to lighten things)*
Yes be on your vigil.

HOLLY *(to Simon)*
Why don't you *shut up*!!!!!!!
If you'd let us use a bloody click track we'd know the tempo and we wouldn't be scurrying around like blind mice trying to figure out what beat we're playing to.

SIMON
What's your problem?

HOLLY
My problem is I'm punching my bloody keys over here and I HAVE NO BLOODY CLUE WHAT THE TEMPO IS.

GROVER *(talkback)*
Do you guys want to take a break //

HOLLY *(bolts up from her seat)*
YOU TELL US!!!!!
ARE WE ON A BREAK OR AREN'T WE!!!
MAKE A BLOODY DECISION!!!!!

Pause.

GROVER *(face reddening; talkback)*
We're . . . taking a break.

Simultaneously: Holly produces a bottle of champagne and pours herself a glass. Peter and Diana give one another a look of bemused defeat and determine the session is over. They make their way out of the studio. Simon fake-stabs himself in the eye with one of his drumsticks, throws the drumsticks down, sighs, and languidly makes his way out of the studio.

Grover shoots Charlie a look.

CHARLIE
What?

GROVER *(to Charlie, loud whisper)*
Shut up.

CHARLIE
I didn't say // anything

GROVER *(loud whisper)*
Shut the fuck up!

Charlie buries his face in his hands. Grover hurriedly exits the control room.

REG *(doing his Cagney impersonation to himself)*
"Nyahhhhh
You dirty rat.
Nyahhhhh . . ."

At this point, it becomes apparent that Holly is the only person in the sound room. She is standing like a caryatid glaring at Reg and sipping her champagne. Reg notices Holly glowering at him and, humiliated, looks away. Holly takes a huge chug of champagne, slams down the glass on her keyboard and exits into the kitchen, slamming the door.

ACT II
FEAR OF MUSIC

1.

They band is mid-rehearsal playing "Seven Roads" (Peter's song from Act I, Scene 2) but in a new arrangement.

PETER

Seven roads
I walked alone
Seven stars
To guide me home
Seven tears I counted in your eye
When I told you all my seven lies

PETER AND DIANA

When you're near
I can't breathe

When you're far
I don't believe

Seven roads I had to journey through
And they always led me back to you

PETER AND DIANA
My love
Ohhhhh oh my love

Peter stops playing, points to Holly, who stops playing. The session breaks down.

Charlie stops the tape machine and marks the track sheet.

PETER *(to Holly)*
I'm not sure about that.
(to Reg)
But I love that
I love that bass line.

REG
Yeah?

PETER
You have to keep that.

Reg plays it again.

REG
I could do this:

He tries something.

Grover checks his watch.

GROVER
I'm supposed to see a movie with Paula.

PETER
That's a little too static. I like it a little // more

REG
Okay //

CHARLIE
Paula? I thought you were boning that waitress.

GROVER
Nah man // she got knocked up

PETER
And can you do the walk up there into the C?

Reg does it.

SIMON
How are the drums there Peter?

PETER
I like that—but can you give it a little more drum?

Simon drums a little bit.
He looks over to Peter.

PETER
Okay but harder.

Simon tries it again, looks at Peter—who's concentrating intensely.
He looks up at Simon.

PETER
Okay so it's you know what it's like?
It's a movie screen.
And it's the middle of summer it's a beautiful day.
We're on the beach.
There are two lovers.
The sun is shining
The waves are sparkling and ebbing.
Then suddenly THERE'S A CUT!
And there's a dead body
And *show* me that dead body with the drums.

Simon is paralyzed but tries to cover.

SIMON
Yeah.

PETER
Show me the *horror* // of

SIMON
Okay //

PETER
Of *shock*
the *shock* of the // disruption

SIMON
Right right

PETER
That's what I want.
so it's:
Boom:
BA *boom* BA boom
Boom:
BA *boom* BA boom

But Simon can't get it.

PETER
Yeah it's
it's still a little harder it's like
BOOM BOOM
and you're still too on the beat.

Simon tries it again.

Short pause.

PETER
Are you okay?

SIMON
Yeah.

PETER
Just try it one more time
you're getting it.
It's just—
it's BOOM BOOM
it's harder.

Simon tries again.

PETER *(to Simon)*
It's better.

SIMON
No, it's not right.

He sets down his drumsticks.

PETER
You wanna take a break?

Simon lifts his drumsticks again.

SIMON
Let's just record.

PETER
Let's try it again. Grover, you recording this?

Grover gives a thumbs-up.
Charlie rolls tape.

PETER
Okay.

He nods to Simon.

Simon counts off with his drumsticks.

The band starts to play. About fifteen seconds in, Simon stops drumming and waves his hand, signaling for the rest of the band to stop.

Charlie stops the tape.

SIMON
Does the drum sound weird to you?

GROVER *(talkback)*
I can hear a slight rattle with the snare.

SIMON *(not hearing him)*
You can what?

GROVER *(talkback)*
The snares are little rattly.

SIMON
The snares are *rattly*?

GROVER *(talkback)*
Yeah it's rattling every time you hit the kick drum.
Hit the kick drum?

Simon hits the kick drum.

SIMON
I don't hear it.

GROVER *(talkback)*
It's rattling.

Simon hits the kick drum again. Again.

SIMON
Oh yeah I hear it.

GROVER *(talkback)*
Hear it?

Then he hits the kick drum some more.

GROVER
Try tightening the snares and tuning up a few lugs.

SIMON
Yeah yeah yeah okay.
Where's the drum key?

He finds the drum key, tightens the snares.
He plays the snares a little bit just to hear it.

SIMON
That fixed it.

He plays it some more.

GROVER *(talkback)*
Play it a little more.

He does.

GROVER *(talkback)*
Now your rack tom
is making your snare drum
sing back at you.

SIMON
What's that?

GROVER *(talkback)*
You brought the snare drum
too close to the rack tom
pitch so now it's
it's resonating back at you.

SIMON
Okay.

GROVER *(talkback)*
So maybe turn your
snare drum back down.

SIMON
You said if I tune it back down
it makes the snares rattle //
when I

GROVER *(talkback)*
No I know.

SIMON
hit the // kick drum

GROVER *(talkback)*
Not all the way back down.

Simon sighs. Turns the snare drum back down.

GROVER *(talkback)*
Okay try it.

Holly pours a glass of champagne. Simon hits the kick drum.

CHARLIE
Now the snare's ringing again.

PETER
What if we use a tea towel . . .
you know, to deaden the tone?

GROVER *(talkback)*
I mean yeah, yeah let's try that.

They get a tea towel, they place it over the snare drum.
Simon plays.

SIMON
It's not quite so crisp, I don't
like that.

GROVER *(talkback)*
Yeah, I hear you.

SIMON
It's too muffled.

GROVER *(talkback)*
Okay what about this?
Try tuning the lugs up a
half a click.

Simon does.

GROVER *(talkback)*
Okay now play.

Simon plays.
He stops.

SIMON
Okay now the snares are
rattling again FUCK!

GROVER *(talkback)*
I didn't hear it that time.
(off talkback) Did you hear it?

CHARLIE
No.

GROVER *(talkback)*
I didn't hear it // that time

Simon stands.

SIMON *(resisting a descent)*
We keep trying to fix it and
it keeps making everything
worse. You know I wish
I hadn't touched it, I really do.
I really do I wish we'd just left
it alone.

GROVER *(walking on eggshells)*
Sorry man.

SIMON *(after a beat)*
A drum is a piece of wood:
A piece. Of wood.
It's ephemeral.
You can't keep changing things.
Now we've changed
everything and I can't
change it back!

GROVER *(talkback)*
Don't freak out, we'll fix it.

SIMON *(forcing a smile)*
Oh, I'm not freaking out
I'm fine.

GROVER
Okay good.

SIMON
It is good.

GROVER
Okay.

SIMON *(not okay)*
It is okay. It's all okay.

He just stares at his drum kit.

GROVER *(talkback)*
What if we //

SIMON *(very quietly)*
Where's my drum key?

GROVER *(talkback)*
Your— //

SIMON
Where's my drum key?
Who took my drum key.

REG
I didn't take it.

PETER
No one took it.

SIMON
Well I just had it where is it.
(waits for someone to respond)
Where is it?

He leaves the room.
After about fifteen seconds:

REG *(to no one in particular)*
Now what?

Diana starts to laugh, tries to keep it in.
Simon comes back, looks around for the drum key.

SIMON
FUCK ALL OF YOU FUCK
EACH AND EVERY ONE
OF YOU
FUCK OFF

He storms out of the sound room.

2.

Just past midnight.
Takeout food lying around.
Everyone looks like zombies,
so tired.

Simon is sitting at his drum, drumming away. He looks like he hasn't slept in a week.

Charlie and Grover are sitting at the console. Peter is sitting at the producer's chair next to them. He's wearing a weird kimono-type thing and odd slippers.

Diana is lying on the floor, holding her crochet needles and some yarn, half asleep.

An exhausted Reg is leaning against a wall doing a yo-yo trick.

Holly is seated on a banquette a few feet away from Reg, flipping through a magazine and smoking a cigarette.

PETER *(to Charlie)*
Pssssst!
Hand me that tape box?

Charlie hands him the tape box. Peter rolls a joint on the tape box.

GROVER
Turn up the speakers.

Charlie turns up the sound room speakers.

GROVER *(talkback)*
Simon?

Simon stops drumming, looks up, jarred.

GROVER *(gingerly)*
How're you doin' out there?

Simon shrugs with both his drumsticks flaring out at the edges.

GROVER
You wanna let me hear the snare?

Simon drums a bit on the snare.

GROVER *(to Peter)*
It sounds fine to me
am I crazy?

PETER *(lost)*
I don't know.

GROVER
This is day six with the
drums. I feel like we're
going down a black hole.

Simon stops.

SIMON
It's a little better?

GROVER *(talkback)*
Yeah . . . yeah.

Simon adjusts his lugs again.
Drums.

Peter lights his joint.
Diana staggers over to Peter at the console, sits on his lap.

DIANA
What are we doing?

Peter rolls his eyes.
He takes a hit, passes the joint to Diana. She takes out her gum and sticks it in the ashtray.
She tokes.

Simon collapses on the drum set.
He stands with his drumsticks and staggers into the control room.

Reg screws up his yo-yo trick, puts the yo-yo down. Sits at the sofa.

SIMON
It's bad, right?

PETER
I don't know man.

Reg makes a talky sound with
his hand and mimics Peter.

PETER
I kinda hear what you're saying but
I can't tell anymore.
Did anyone go in the sound room
or touch anything?

SIMON
No idea.

PETER
We gotta
We gotta be really vigilant.

Reg makes a talky sound with his hand.

PETER *(just catching Reg)*
No one can—*stop*
that, please? No one can
come in here.

CHARLIE
No one's allowed in.

GROVER
We'll get it right.

Reg stands, produces a salad.
He unwraps it from a crinkly,
somewhat loud paper bag over:

GROVER
Maybe it's the mics.

SIMON
It's not the mics.

GROVER
Okay let me just try something.

Grover runs into the sound room.
Simon follows.

Charlie cracks open a beer.
Reg sits next to Charlie at the console.

Grover moves the mics around.

CHARLIE
You want // one?

SIMON
I hate moving these bloody mics // around

Simon sits at the drum kit while Grover futzes with the mics.

REG
No thank you, I prefer freshly squeezed juice. I don't drink anymore, Charlie. Got a number-one record now. We're a number-one band. I'm turning over a new leaf.

SIMON
It's all we ever bloody do
Moving the // bloody mics

CHARLIE
Oh yeah?

SIMON
I don't think it's the mics
(does the kick drum)

Reg unseals a small packet, dissolves some powder into a mug.

Grover continues to reposition the mic. Simon plays the drums for a bit.

Charlie mutes the volume in the sound room.

CHARLIE
What's that?

REG
That's powder
it gives you energy.

CHARLIE
What about cocaine?
That's powder
it gives you energy.

REG
Cocaine isn't natural.

CHARLIE
It's from plants.

REG
I went to that shop near
The Triangle

the all-natural shop?
And everything fresh
See?
I got me grains and seeds.
I've got me wheat germ
freshly ground peanut butter
and sliced carrots
shredded carrots
bean sprouts
tahini dressing . . .

CHARLIE
Nice.

REG
Peas
snap peas
when was the last time
you had a salad?
I'll bet you can't remember—
grape nuts!
You never get sick eating all
this.

CHARLIE
Oh wow.

Grover peeks his head into the control room.

GROVER
Peter can you come in here?

Peter goes to the sound room. Grover and Peter huddle around Simon with their hands on their hips.

Diana watches them briefly, then
puts her head in her hands.

DIANA
Oh my god.

She laughs bleakly for a moment.
She turns off the speakers.

Holly shuts her magazine, sidles
over to Reg and Charlie.

REG
Did you know that some parts of
the pine tree are edible?
But we throw it away.
We're wasting everything.
Wasting our lives
wasting our souls and hearts.
There's all this negative energy
but we've got to get the positive energy
to flow through us.
Positive energy flows more readily
through me when I eat a vegetarian diet

HOLLY
Salad's nice, it keeps you in shape.

REG *(smiling to himself)*
Yeah.

Reg smiles. Holly runs her fingers through Reg's
hair, gives him a flirty smile.

HOLLY
Keep me having a nice figure my salad.

Diana clocks all this, makes a face.
Holly pours a glass of champagne,
sashays to the sofa and sits.
She looks over at Reg, who crunches a
bit of salad, winks. Diana marches over to
the sofa, sits next to Holly, gives her a look.

DIANA
What:
is going on?

Holly smirks, wiggles her eyebrows.

DIANA
What?!

Holly wiggles her eyebrows again.
Diana laughs, shakes her head.

Grover peeks his head into the
control room.

GROVER
Hey can you guys come in here
a sec?

He goes back into the sound room.
Charlie follows Grover into the
sound room.

Reg follows Charlie, carrying his
salad with him.

Now there are four people standing around with their hands on their hips watching Simon try different things with the drum. Every so often someone adjusts a peg, then they go back to standing and looking.

DIANA *(quietly despairing)*
How long have we been here?

HOLLY
Where?

DIANA
Simon said it would only take
a month // tops

HOLLY
What?

DIANA
The *record.*

HOLLY
Oh
well it's been . . .

DIANA
What month is this?

HOLLY
What month?

DIANA
Yeah.

Holly struggles to answer. Her inability
strikes Diana as absolutely hilarious.
Which makes Holly laugh.
They're both insanely slaphappy.
After a bit, the laughter dwindles.
Then—back to the drudgery of waiting around.

DIANA
I'm so tired.
I thought I would sleep better
now but I still get insomnia
even with ludes I'm like this in bed:
(she makes a face like a zombie)
and then at eleven I have a hit
of coke and I'm like
(she makes a face of frozen excitement)
I really should be dead;
I don't actually know how I'm
still living. No really
I don't know the name of what I'm singing
or how to tune a guitar . . .
(beat)
We have a number-one *album*
and I don't know how to turn the knobs
on the amps It's ridiculous.
(beat)
I can't be a rock star and be this stupid.

HOLLY
Can I lie down on your lap?

DIANA
You want to lie down on my lap?
Yes baby you can lie down // I just

HOLLY *(lying down)*
Oh thank you //

DIANA
I just have to move my yarn and
make sure I don't jab you with
this needle Otherwise you'll have a
needle in your face.

HOLLY *(getting snuggly)*
I want a needle in my face
Put me out of my misery.

DIANA
You have to teach me keyboard.

HOLLY
You need to play Bach
Bach develops your left hand.

DIANA
How?

HOLLY
Because you do a lot of this:
(does a thing with her left hand)

DIANA
I can do that.

HOLLY *(delightful realization)*
I'm nearly halfway to being drunk.

DIANA
Well I'll tell you one thing:
I've got to expand my repertoire
because guess what:

I am running out of tools in my toolbox
and it's getting to be really a drag.
(short pause)
I think we're really famous.

HOLLY
Yeah.

DIANA
No I'm not kidding
We're *famous*
I went to the gynecologist on Saturday
And I had my legs in the stirrups and he
asked me for an autograph.
(Holly laughs)
I was like, um, I'm kind of busy right now.

HOLLY
Fame is strange
None of my famous friends like it.

DIANA
And someone told me that if you're famous
you can only be friends with other famous people
I'm not doing that.

HOLLY
Be friends with me!

DIANA *(cheeky)*
Okay—I only need one friend.
(Holly laughs)
Oh wait I screwed this up
(fixes her crochet stitch)
Actually my friend Lana said she was
coming up next week.

HOLLY
Oh she's nice.

Holly pours another drink.

HOLLY
Did I ever tell you what they named me
when I played organ for the church?

DIANA
What?

HOLLY
"Shy Little Girl."

DIANA
Shy Little *Girl*?
That was a stage name?
(Holly nods. Diana makes a face)
How old were you?

HOLLY
Well it started when I was what—
thirteen, fourteen?

DIANA
That's not even that little!

HOLLY
I // know

DIANA
I had my period when I was eleven,
are you kidding me?

HOLLY
They wanted a little girl.
And I never felt I became a woman
because they wanted a little girl.
You get stuck in these ways of
thinking about yourself, you know.

Diana thinks on this a moment.

DIANA
Yeah.
(snaps out of it)
I'm sorry—"Shy Little *Girl*"?
Your parents let them *do* that?

HOLLY
Well I really was shy.
I wouldn't look anyone in the eye,
I found it absolutely // unbearable

DIANA
And see I would never say that you
were a shy person.

HOLLY
Because I hide it—because I'm ashamed
of my shyness, or // you know—

DIANA
No no it makes sense; I have this
fight with Peter all the time, that I'm
shy, and he tells me that I'm not shy,
and I go well yes I'm *expressive*,
but I'm also *retreating* at the same time,
and— *(beat)* He doesn't understand true shyness.

HOLLY
This is why I hide behind my little keyboard
because I get scared.

DIANA
I get scared too.

HOLLY
I know you do.

Diana crochets for a while.
Holly drinks, smokes for a bit.

HOLLY *(cynical)*
I know what you're thinking.

DIANA
I'm not thinking anything.

HOLLY
Yeah you are.

DIANA *(laughing)*
No, I'm not.

HOLLY *(dead certainty)*
You are so judgmental.

DIANA
What are you talking about?

HOLLY
A relationship
any relationship is a series of negotiations.
I was naive, I didn't understand that
before but that's what it is.

You're negotiating to get something
and in return you give something
and *that's* the bargain.
(pause)
Do you judge me?

DIANA
Have I ever judged you?

HOLLY
Well I'm very square so— No I am,
I was raised to believe marriage
was for life And I guess I believe that.
(pause)
When I first met you and
Peter, I think I idealized your relationship.

DIANA
Really?

HOLLY
You were hippies, you grew your own pot.
And you sewed those
those little moons and stars onto his jeans.

DIANA
Well he wanted that.
The whole wifey wifey thing He
still wants it.

Pause.

HOLLY
I put everything in compartments,
that's my problem.

I used to think if you're in love, it should just
feel one way, it should be one thing.
But nothing's like that, is it?

DIANA *(far-off)*
No . . . I guess not.

Diana has entered into a dreamy,
almost trancelike state.

DIANA
I had this crazy dream
The night before I found out
about *Billboard*?
In the dream I was doing my makeup
in the mirror in my
old apartment on Laveta Terrace.
And, like all of a sudden my face wasn't really
my face anymore
it was a mask.
(beat)
And the mask started to glow and
expand, it started to
not be me anymore.
And it got bigger and bigger and
there was this crazy terrifying
mask face staring at me.
(pause)
And when I woke up
I went to the bathroom and threw up.
And the next morning we had
a number-one album.

3.

The studio is slightly dark now,
a little bit in a twilight.
Mood lighting.

Meters moving on the console.
Red lights bouncing.

The band recording the end of Diana's song from Act I, Scene 3 ("Bright") in a brand-new arrangement.

DIANA
The nighttime loves you
But it's not your friend
The lights will flicker
And we're lost again

The crowd is laughing
But the joke, it isn't clear
I want to click my heels
and disappear but

DIANA, PETER AND HOLLY
I'm in the bright light

DIANA
Forgetting my name

DIANA, PETER AND HOLLY
The shadow of our lives

DIANA
Familiar but strange
Not enough darkness left to
Hide all the pain

DIANA, PETER AND HOLLY
I'm in the bright light again
I'm in the bright light again
I'm in the bright light again
I'm in the bright light again

Song finishes.

Charlie stops the tape.

GROVER *(talkback)*
That sounded great. I think we got it. It's almost two, do you guys wanna call it a night?

SIMON
Yeah let's call it a night, I'm knackered.

GROVER *(talkback)*
Get home safe everybody.
See you tomorrow at noon.

They start packing to leave. Holly stands, moves to Diana, wraps her arm around her, gives her shoulder a squeeze. They whisper back and forth, mainly inaudible. Reg joins them—he's being quite flirty and physical with Holly.

Charlie organizes a bunch of loose pages, etc. Grover opens a beer. Simon enters the control room. He is rooting around for something.

Peter is standing, transfixed, deep in concentration.

SIMON
Where's my keys?
(he finds them)
Cheerio, boys!

He scoops up his keys, salutes Grover and Charlie and leaves the studio.

Peter doing music math in his head. He's inaudibly fingering his guitar, very focused. After a beat:

PETER *(to the band)*
Wait—wait wait I have an idea
(he moves up to the window)
Grover don't go anywhere.

GROVER *(talkback)*
I'm here.

PETER
Did Simon leave already?

GROVER *(talkback)*
He just left.

PETER
See if you can catch him?

Charlie goes after Simon.

Holly sits back behind the piano. Diana waits at the mic.

Simon, Reg and Charlie reenter.

Simon enters the sound room.

PETER
Can we just try one thing?
I had an idea.

SIMON *(sits at his drum kit)*
Yeah.

Peter squeezes his temples with his palms, shuts his eyes like he's casting a spell.

PETER
Okay. Simon, let's pull out the fill on this. Do four on the floor.

Simon starts to play.

PETER
Reg, can you now hit the floor?

Reg nods, starts to play.

PETER
And then I wanna take the whole thing and slow it way down. Take it down 20 BPM.

GROVER *(talkback)*
Okay great, you wanna try it?

DIANA
I liked it before.

PETER
We can always go back.
I just wanna take a look at this.
(to the band)
Let's take it from the third verse.

GROVER *(talkback)*
Everyone ready?

Peter nods.

Charlie gets the tape ready, nods to Grover.

GROVER *(talkback)*
Wheels up.
"Bright," take 21.

Charlie presses record. Meters moving. Red lights bouncing.

They start playing.

DIANA
You've been singing
In your sleep again
But the words come out all—

PETER *(shakes his head)*
No. No.

They stop playing.
Then, after a moment:

PETER
Let's try it with just the piano.

HOLLY
Okay.

PETER *(to Diana)*
Actually you should play on this. *(to Holly)* Is that okay?

Holly nods and gets back on keyboard.

DIANA *(vaguely annoyed)*
Peter I don't play.

PETER
Yeah but I don't want it to be all polished. Let's just try it.

Diana rolls her eyes, laughs, exhausted. She goes reluctantly to the piano, sits, stares at the keys for a moment.

GROVER
"Bright," take 22.

Diana starts to play. Holly extemporaneously begins to complement Diana on the keyboard. At some point, Peter joins in with guitar as the song builds and builds into something thrilling.

DIANA

You've been singing
In your sleep again
But the words come out all
cluttered
I can't make sense
Like you're dreaming of a love
song
But what good is love
When the wind starts blowing?
Nothing forgotten nothing
forgiven
When the night comes to an end
Like a child you hold out your
hand and tremble
Like I'm right beside you
And not a million miles away

DIANA, PETER AND HOLLY

I'm in the bright light

DIANA

Forgetting my name

DIANA, PETER AND HOLLY

The shadow of our lives

DIANA

Familiar but strange
Without enough darkness left to

PETER, DIANA AND HOLLY

Hide all the pain
I'm in the bright light again

DIANA

The nighttime loves you but it's
not your friend
The lights will flicker and we're
lost again
The crowd is laughing
But the joke, it isn't clear
I want to click my heels and
disappear but

DIANA, PETER AND HOLLY

I'm in the bright light

DIANA

Forgetting my name

DIANA, PETER AND HOLLY

The shadow of our lives

DIANA

Familiar but strange
Without enough darkness left to

PETER, DIANA AND HOLLY

Hide all the pain

DIANA

I'm in the bright light again
I'm in the bright light again
I'm in the bright light again
I'm in the bright light again

I'm in the bright light again
I'm in the bright light again

PETER, DIANA, SIMON AND HOLLY
I'm in the bright light again

DIANA
I'm in the bright light again

When they finish, a moment of stunned silence. Peter smiles a little Cheshire Cat smile. He looks over at Diana.

Charlie stops the tape.

PETER
What do you think?

Diana just starts laughing and covers her face. She's close to tears. She walks over to Peter, clasps his hands in hers.

DIANA
It's great.

PETER *(barreling through)*
It's good but there's only so much I can do if you're not gonna cut the verses down; your ego is getting in the way And you need to decide if you're gonna be a mediocre songwriter or push it to the next level.

(beat)
But that's up to you.

Simon rolls his eyes.
Diana masks her humiliation
with a tiny smile.

GROVER *(talkback)*
Let's visit this tomorrow
I think we're all pretty beat.

PETER
Yep.

A miffed Simon exits quickly.

Charlie and Grover are dealing
with track sheets, taking notes.

Peter puts his guitar away,
exits to control room.

Reg goes over, confabulates with
Diana and Holly briefly.

Peter sits down at the console,
rolls a joint while Charlie and
Grover speak sotto voce.

PETER
Why don't you guys just leave?
it's so late.
Good work today. I'll close
up shop.

CHARLIE
Thanks Peter.

GROVER
Thanks Peter.

They get their coats, get ready to go.

*Diana enters the control room,
sits on Peter's lap, watches him roll
the joint.*

*Holly and Reg enter shortly thereafter,
mid-singing.*

REG *(sings Aretha Franklin)*
"*Chain chain chaaaa // aaaain*"

*Grover and Charlie exit in
quiet conversation.*

HOLLY
No it's "*chaaaaa // aaaaaain*"

REG
No it's "*chaaaaa // aaaaain*"

HOLLY *(refuting him playfully)*
"*chaaaaain*"

REG *(playing with her)*
Oh really is that what you think?

HOLLY *(playing)*
Yeah in fact that is // what I think

REG
Oh is that how you're gonna be now,
alright I see // how it is

HOLLY
No I don't think you do see.

REG
Get over here.

He grabs her around the waist. She starts tickling him.

HOLLY
No you get over here.

He grabs her wrists, holds them behind her back. He pulls her toward him. Reg and Holly kiss. A really intense, beautiful kiss.

Diana has been staring at them this whole time, smiling and watching how they are as a couple. Reg and Holly finish kissing, they hold hands, swinging arms.

REG *(softly)*
You wanna go?

They grab their coats.

HOLLY *(to Peter and Diana)*
G'night.

Holly waves at Peter and Diana. Peter and Diana wave back. Holly and Reg exit holding hands.

Diana watches Peter roll the joint.

DIANA
I'm not cutting the verses down.
(beat)
It's not your song Peter.

PETER
Okay.

DIANA
You have to stop criticizing me so much.
I need you to be a little nicer to me
at least in front of the band.

PETER
I *am* nice // to you

DIANA
Peter I have no self-confidence
I can't *not* have self-confidence and
get up on stage in front of
ten thousand people
and be a rock star.
I can't do it,
you need to help me out here.

PETER
I can't give you self-confidence.

DIANA
I know that and I'm not asking for that
I just
(pause)
If you could just . . . please // just

PETER
Okay
I'm sorry if I'm doing that.

DIANA
Yeah
Thank you, I // just

PETER
It's not deliberate.

DIANA
I need—I know it's not—I just need
a little encouragement
Sometimes.

PETER
I'll try to encourage you more.

DIANA
Or at least some space to just—
I just
I don't like when you say stuff
in front of the band.

PETER
Okay but I need to be able to speak openly
If I'm feeling something in the room
I need to say it.

DIANA
I know.

PETER
I can't lie to // you

DIANA
I don't want you to lie
but you don't have to do—*this:*
(she pokes a few times at him)

You know?
It's not like I don't know how
to push your buttons Peter.
Just because I don't unravel the thread
doesn't mean I don't know where it *is*.
But when you love someone
you don't do that.

PETER
I think you romanticize who you are
a little bit.
You're looking out for yourself
just as much as I do;
you're very ambitious.

DIANA
I'm not *ambitious*,
don't sling mud at me.

PETER
You wanna use me to arrange a song
but then when I'm telling you it's too long
or to cut something
you have no interest
and then you take it as a criticism
then don't ask me to // arrange a song

DIANA
Because you can be very aggressive Peter!

PETER
How am // I

DIANA
I don't like to be *forced*
okay?

I'll do it but in my own time
I don't like to be forced;
now:
I will *do* what you ask of me
I will *do* it
but as I said //

PETER
You don't like to be // forced

DIANA
Well I // don't

PETER
But you did this // when

DIANA
No hold // on

PETER
You did this from back in 1968
when you hated The Beatles because
I was telling you to listen to The Beatles
you know, I // was

DIANA
No no no.

PETER
For *form*—

DIANA
No
That's

look I'll *do* it
my thing is always why do you
have to force me?

PETER
But see // I

DIANA
But that's my main like
sort of question like
I will do it?
I will come to it?
I'm passionate
I care You *know* I care
Everyone knows how much I care,
I am *into this*, I am committed so *why*
do you feel the need to *move* my hand
and *force* my hand
and control every single thing I do
until there's no joy in it
there's no discovery
anywhere
there's nothing spontaneous.

PETER
Right.

DIANA
Because then I'm just not interested
I don't have goose bumps or excitement
I'm just a puppet
and if I'm a // puppet?

PETER
That's not what I // want

DIANA
There's no // joy in it—

PETER
I don't want a puppet
I want you engaged
and happy and all that
and
I think you're tremendous as an artist
and a songwriter and a singer
which you also know because
I tell // you all the—

DIANA
I can hear it more often to be honest.

PETER
Well I'm telling you now.

He kisses her hand.

DIANA
Oh boy—going for the hand . . .
(beat)
I love chivalry. I love when
you get like this
(beat)
Look at your face
You remind me of Mooch, my dog
I told you about Mooch, when I was seven?

PETER *(disgruntled)*
Yeah Mooch.

DIANA
He used to get very, like this with his neck,
when he felt betrayed or if we
left him alone too long, his spine
would like get very erect like a monarch,
he wanted us to *know* how profound
his feelings were, which they were,
because animals are profound.

PETER
Okay so—I don't understand,
we were having a romantic—
(Diana cracks up—which makes him laugh)
. . . and now we're talking about your *dog*?
Can we // like

DIANA
No—come on—it's so sweet, that's all.

PETER
Yeah
well you're sweet.

He kisses her.

PETER
I love you baby.

Her mind is suddenly racing at one hundred miles an hour—it's like his kiss opened up some psychological Pandora's box.

DIANA
And then I have all this other
stuff // eating away at

PETER
What //

DIANA
me, things I could never tell you, or
things I want to avoid telling you //

PETER *(not super into this)*
Okay //

DIANA
Because I thought I was getting things out
with the music because it's so expressive and
exhausting but you *don't.*
You *can't* get it all out that way,
even though it feels like you do,
it's just a trick, all the conflict gets like
submerged and hidden in some other
weird pocket of your psyche
and you think you had a
catharsis onstage at Madison Square Garden
and it's like, oh, no, that wasn't a catharsis,
that was a *character*, but what about *me*?

PETER
Well—

DIANA
And like when you sold my guitar.

PETER
Okay
That was seven years // ago

DIANA
The guitar that
took me *months* and *months* to save for.

PETER
The guitar you used *literally once*.

DIANA
But that wasn't right.

PETER
Because you didn't do the work!

DIANA
That wasn't—and that's still
That whole heavy dynamic between us is still
very present and alive.

Peter smiles, shaking his head, shrugging.

DIANA
Don't shake your head.

PETER
What are you doing?
Why are you // talking about

DIANA
Because Peter
I was gonna—I would have learned
the electric guitar
okay?
And you were right, I wasn't practicing enough
I wasn't doing all the things you told me to do

I was working at that stupid old folks' home and
changing people's diapers so we could make *rent*.
But I was still planning on—
and I was never gonna be Keith Richards
I was never gonna be Jimmy Page
but I was still planning on learning it
to give myself some kind of—of, of *literacy*!
And then suddenly my guitar is *gone*.
And then I'm being *forced* again and
now I'm playing this fucking *triangle*
and I'm onstage
doing *this (does a thing)* with my hands
because I have nothing
to do with my hands
because I can't *play an instrument*
because I *am still messed up*
from you *selling my stuff*!

Pause.

PETER
Okay: I didn't *make* you get that // job,
You *wanted* to—NO YOU wanted to get that

DIANA
No but you—

PETER
job, you said *No* Peter *you* should be writing songs,
I'll work. And you *made* that money and I *wrote* those
songs and *that's* why we're here.
That demo got us *this* gig that
got you your number-one *fucking* song.

DIANA *(quietly)*
You're right . . .

PETER
I just
I think sometimes you take these things
out on me
like you're rebelling // against

DIANA
I never rebelled.

PETER
But I think—

DIANA
I never rebelled I was always a good girl //

PETER
But that's exactly it, I think you rebel against *me*;
you're looking for something to push
against and I'm the closest to you

DIANA *(thinks on it)*
That might be true //

PETER
I think it is true.

DIANA
But *Peter*?
You never rebelled *either*.

PETER
I rebelled.

DIANA
No you did not.

PETER
I rebelled covertly.

DIANA
Oh
That makes sense.

PETER
I hid my rebellion, I did it on // the side

DIANA
But your dad pushed you so hard
and you—you can't have kids and
be that way because then they'll turn out
you know . . . like *you.*

PETER *(smiling but a little hurt)*
That's mean.

DIANA
I mean intense //

PETER
I don't know
I thought my dad did a good job.

DIANA *(gobsmacked that he would think that)*
He did *not* do a good job.

PETER
Well, Brian is hugely successful—
and *I'm* doing okay // I mean

DIANA
But you and Brian, your dad
ripped up that relationship,
you haven't spoken to // Brian since

PETER
Well there's that competition, yeah
but there's always been that,
that's not Dad's fault //

DIANA *(duhhhh)*
Peter!

PETER
What

DIANA
Yes it is
it *is* his fault: he pit you and Brian
against each other you won't even
go in the water now because you
feel like a failure
that's what you said to me—
even Stinson *Beach*—

PETER *(still tiny smile, but more hurt)*
So you don't think I'd be a good dad?
Is that why you won't have kids with me?

DIANA
I did not say that.

PETER
Well then why won't you have a baby with me?
(pause)
We've been together nine years.
Nine.
Years.

Short pause.

DIANA
We just got out of that other fight
You really want to have *this* fight?

PETER
Yeah I do.

DIANA
Okay well where am I having this baby?
Like on *stage*?
We have a tour coming up
we're cutting an album //

PETER
Fuck the album.

DIANA
Peter.

PETER
I'm just // saying

DIANA
We have a number-one record
this doesn't just happen to people
I // mean

PETER
I think it'll make us closer.

DIANA
No: you'll feel close to *me*,
but I will hate you and I will resent you
and it will ruin us Is that what you want?

PETER
It won't ruin us.

DIANA
You'll be fine. *My* life will be ruined!
We'll have a screaming baby
I'll be tripping all over my breast milk—

Pause.

PETER
See this is how it works with you
"I'm forcing you I'm forcing you"
But if I don't force you to have a baby
it's not like you're going to come around.
You won't.

Silence.

PETER
What are you thinking?

Pause.

DIANA *(tired)*
That I'm being forced again.

Peter buries his head in his hands.
There's a long pause.

PETER
I'll see you at the house.

DIANA
I'm meeting Holly at Juanita's.

He picks up his guitar and plays the riff.

PETER
Okay.

He plays.

DIANA
You can come.

He ignores her. She stands there
for a while but he's going to ignore her.

DIANA
I'll see you at the house.

She exits. He plays alone in the studio.

4.

The band is laying down tracks for Peter's song "Masquerade."

PETER
Got my ticket to the Masquerade

Grover signals from the booth.

The song breaks down.

GROVER *(talkback)*
You guys it's good but you need to watch the tempo—it's getting a little slow.

SIMON *(to Grover)*
What's that?

GROVER *(talkback)*
Tempo.

SIMON
Uh-huh
Uh-huh
Tempo yeah.
(drums)
Okay.
(drums)

GROVER
Okay we're rolling.
"Masquerade," take 33.

They all start playing.

GROVER *(to Charlie)*
It's muddy.

CHARLIE
Yeah.

He listens some more.

GROVER *(talkback)*
Holly, you and Peter are
playing in the same register.
Can you move one up
or down?

HOLLY
I'll try different voicing.

She tries another set of chords.

HOLLY
Is that better?

GROVER *(talkback)*
Yeah, better.

SIMON
How was the tempo?

GROVER *(talkback)*
It dragged.

SIMON
It dragged?

GROVER *(talkback)*
Yeah you really sagged a little bit there. Do you want to use the click track?

SIMON *(dry, a little nasty)*
Do I want to use a *click track*? I don't need a click track, Grover. No. No I don't.

GROVER *(talkback)*
I think it might make things easier.

SIMON
Let's do it again. I'll get it right.

GROVER *(talkback)*
Okay stand by. We're rolling. "Masquerade," take 34.

They play for a bit; it starts to slow down again.

GROVER *(to Charlie)*
What is going *on*?

Charlie shrugs, confounded, exhausted. Stops the tape.

GROVER *(talkback)*
It's getting slower and slower—it's like a funeral dirge guys, pick it up.

SIMON
It didn't feel slower //

HOLLY
Well it was! Just use the bloody click track.

SIMON
Who asked you!

HOLLY
Just *use it*!

SIMON
I don't *need. It.* It's *distracting* to me. Just mind your own business.

Pause.

GROVER *(talkback)*
Let's take it from the top. "Masquerade," take 35.

They start over, but this time Simon is super energized.

Charlie looks at Grover and starts laughing. He stops the tape.

GROVER *(talkback)*
Okay, now it's like a polka. Just slow it down a little bit? "Masquerade," take 36.

They start again.

Grover is losing it.

GROVER
Fuck me.
(sighs; then to Charlie)
Put in the click track.
(talkback)

Uh, guys? Okay that was
great but it's still a little slow.
We're gonna use the click track.

Simon stands—full on umbrage.

SIMON
I said I don't need it, Grover.

GROVER *(talkback)*
We're using // it

SIMON
I don't need a bloody *click track.*

GROVER *(talkback)*
The tempo is sucking really
bad and you do need it.

Simon bolts up from his seat.

SIMON
Who the *fuck* do you think
you're talking to?

GROVER *(talkback)*
The tempo is completely
thrown off
and we don't have time
to waste on this.
It's three in the fucken
morning. We're
using the click track.

*A standoff. Simon looks like he
might blow up.*

GROVER *(talkback; gentler)*
The drum sounds great but
the tempo is off.

*Tense pause—it could go either
way. Simon sits back down. He
sighs—it's a slight concession.*

Charlie takes this as a signal to play the click track.

GROVER *(talkback)*
Can you hear it?

SIMON
Uh-huh.

GROVER
Okay let's take it from the top. "Masquerade," take 37.

PETER
Got my ticket to the masquerade
My soul is sold and the money paid
I've been hearing so long
That's where you had gone
So I grabbed my bag and I'm on my way

Grover's bopping and grooving. His idea works brilliantly.

PETER, DIANA AND HOLLY
The old man said that I shouldn't go
Said there were things I couldn't know

PETER
I said you may be wise
But you haven't seen her eyes

PETER, DIANA AND HOLLY
He just shook his head and
I hit the road
Why why why why

PETER
Why won't the sun rise?

PETER, DIANA AND HOLLY
Why why why why

PETER
Why can't I forget your eyes

PETER AND DIANA
The shadows reaching out for my
heart
But I keep moving on through
the dark

PETER
I'd love to stop a while
I've traveled many miles

PETER, DIANA AND HOLLY
But nothing, child, gonna keep
us apart
Why why why why

PETER
Why won't the sun rise

PETER AND DIANA
Why why why why

PETER
Why can't I forget your eyes
The promises I made
Were made of glass
I gathered all the shards to bring
to you

PETER, DIANA AND HOLLY

I lit a candle and I prayed for forty nights

PETER

I haven't heard an answer yet

PETER, DIANA AND HOLLY

I like the silence anyway
Got my ticket to the masquerade
My soul is sold and the money paid

PETER

The road is long and thin
And the world is full of sin

PETER, DIANA AND HOLLY

But I got my gun and I'm on my way
I'll see you when I get there
I'm gonna see you when I get there
I'll see you when I get there
I'm gonna see you when I get there
I'll see you when I get there
I'm gonna see you when I get there

They finish the song.

GROVER *(on talkback)*

Guys, it sounds fucking great—

REG

I felt really good about it.

DIANA
I did too.

REG
That felt great.

GROVER *(talkback)*
Do you want to come in and have a listen?

SIMON *(a little kid)*
YES!!!!! YES GROVER YES!!!

He does a little dance at his drum set and then sprints out of the room using his drumsticks as extempore ski poles. They all bound out of the room, all gossipy and giggly like little kids.

Charlie rewinds the tape, plays it back.

HOLLY
The bass sounds amazing.

DIANA
I love the bass Reg—wow.

REG
Thank you.

Diana kisses him on the forehead. They listen some more.

PETER
It sounds fucking great.

SIMON *(pulls everyone in for a huddle)*
WE'RE SUCH A GOOD BAND!!!

Grover starts laughing. Reg pulls in Holly and starts doing a groovy dance.
Diana dances over to Peter—they start dancing and smooching like teenagers.
They're all dancing and laughing like kids.

ACT III
WISH YOU WERE HERE

1.

In the darkness. Bouncing red lights on the console. Tape moving.

Diana at a mic in the sound room—singing a verse of "East of Eden."

The studio is dotted with Christmas ornaments.
Grover, Charlie and Peter at the console. Grover is playing with isolated tracks over the singing.
Then no tracks—just the vocal.
Then tracks surging back in.

DIANA
To the east of Eden
Flowers in my hair
Stumble from the garden

I didn't even care
Why do you still refuse me?
Kindness is crawling after you
Why do we have to choose when
Everything you got is right in
front of—

The music keeps going.

Grover stops the tape.

DIANA
I couldn't get the note.
Sorry let's just go from
(singing)
Why do we // da da da

GROVER
Okay I'll punch you in.

He presses record.
The red lights go on the console.

DIANA
Why do we have to choose when
Everything you got is right in
front of you—

PETER *(talkback)*
Do that line again.

DIANA
Which.

PETER *(sings)*
"Everything you // got—"

DIANA
When everything you got is ba //
ba ba—

PETER *(talkback)*
You're doing a G-sharp there.

DIANA
What's that?

PETER *(talkback)*
It used to be a B—right on that line, you—it was // a B

DIANA
Oh //

PETER *(talkback)*
And it turned into a G-sharp somehow.

DIANA
Really?
(to herself)
Everything you—
(hums it)
Okay //

PETER *(talkback)*
That's a B //

DIANA
Okay sorry
you're right.

PETER *(talkback)*
"Everything // you—"

DIANA
"*Everything you* da da da . . ."
okay I got it
I got it now; I'll get it.

PETER *(talkback)*
Okay try it again?

GROVER *(talkback)*
Can you get a little closer to the mic?

DIANA
Okay, but like
I'm eating the mic at // this
point—

GROVER *(talkback)*
I know but the closer . . .
The closer // you

DIANA
What?

GROVER *(talkback)*
Huh? No, I was just saying
the closer you get to the mic
the more bottom I can get out
of the vocal . . . and then
I can control it with the EQ.

PETER *(to Grover)*
Can you comp something
together from those
other takes?

GROVER
We have the take
We just need to fix this one spot.

PETER
You can't comp it?

GROVER
No this is the section man.
This is the problem.
We could revisit it tomorrow.

PETER
We're not revisiting shit.

Diana sings the lyric, hums it a bit.

PETER *(to Grover)*
She's really ringy, Jesus.

DIANA
Sorry.
(she clears her throat)

PETER *(talkback)*
What's up?

DIANA
Where's the Courvoisier?

She gets it—as she pours in some honey and lemon:

PETER *(talkback)*
Do you want to change the key?

DIANA
Peter, I'll get it.

PETER
Well we've been here a long // time

DIANA *(not reactive)*
Yeah I'm
having trouble hitting the note.

PETER
It's not just the note
There was some sloppiness with the line too.

DIANA
Well I'm trying to sing it.
(pause)
I mean I'm standing at a microphone I'm singing it
I'm trying to sing it.

Diana sighs and looks down at the floor for a bit. She laughs a little to herself.

PETER
It's *your* song
I'm trying to help // *you*

DIANA
Can you just help me?

PETER
I *am* helping you.
(to Grover) God, she's on a tear.

DIANA
I'm having trouble hitting the note.
(silence)
Just give me a second.

Grover resets.

GROVER *(to Peter)*
We're running out of tracks.
If you wanna keep all of these takes I'm gonna need to get a new reel.

PETER
Yeah yeah okay.

GROVER
At some point
I'm gonna have to start bouncing things
we're running out of room.

PETER
Yeah we're gonna need to throw out some bad // ideas

DIANA
Okay, let's go //

GROVER *(talkback)*
Okay we're ready.

Diana begins to lay the vocal down again.

DIANA
Why do we have to choose when
Everything you—

She can't hit the note.

Charlie stops the tape machine.

There's a weird, awful silence where she just stands there.

PETER *(talkback)*
Let's just try it in a different key //

DIANA
You're getting in my *head*, and I can't do the song like this. *(beat)* I can't enter the song because I'm getting so in my head You're telling me too many things //

PETER
I'm telling you *one* thing. I'm giving you *one* note Can you not take a single note?

DIANA
I'm just getting in my head.

PETER
Then don't get in your own head. Be a professional.

Pause.

DIANA
I *am* a professional.

PETER
Okay.

DIANA
Just help me with this.

PETER
Do you want help? Or
do you want me to shut up?
You're just standing with your
hand on your hip
Everything is just a pose
with you.

DIANA
I'm standing like this because
I'm exhausted.

PETER
I don't like the way you're
speaking to me right now.

She closes her eyes from sheer exhaustion.

DIANA
Look there's
There's a constructive way of
doing this and there is an
unconstructive way and you //
keep

PETER
That's not a word.

DIANA
What? //

PETER
"Unconstructive," that's // not a

DIANA
I DON'T CARE IF IT'S A WORD!

Peter buries his head in his hands.

Silence.

DIANA
Can I talk to you privately?

PETER
No.

Pause.

DIANA
Okay
Well we need to talk
right now so come in here.

Peter sighs.
Charlie gives Grover a look.

Diana takes off the cans.
Peter goes in the sound room.
She slashes a finger across the neck—a sign to engineers to shut off the sound. Diana takes Peter's hand, leads him away from sightlines into an iso booth.

Charlie goes to turn the sound off but Grover stops him.
They listen in.

DIANA
I know you're really angry
with me // but

PETER
You need to trust me.

DIANA
Yeah but // Peter

PETER
No
You need to trust me
Okay?
And you need to take the ego
Out of it.

DIANA
You need to take the ego out of it not me. I'm not the one bringing—

PETER *(whispering, furious)*
Well then what do you call this you're calling a private fucking // meeting

DIANA
Because // you're

PETER
in the middle of overdubs
what do you call that?
I'm producing the fucking album.

Pause.

DIANA *(in tears)*
The way we work has to
change.

Beat.

PETER
Okay, so we'll change the way
we work.

DIANA
But we *can't* change it!

Beat.

PETER
We'll work on it.

Beat.

DIANA *(a realization)*
We can't work on it, Peter.
(pause)
I think this is over.

Grover shakes his head, throws his head back in exasperation.

GROVER
Nonononono.

PETER
Okay
well I'm producing the record.

DIANA
I'm not talking about the
record.

GROVER *(loud whisper)*
Shit.

Pause.

PETER
You can't bring our stuff in here
You can't do that.

Beat.

DIANA
Peter I can't breathe.
(beat)
No no—no no no // don't

PETER
Okay.

DIANA
Don't touch me—I just

We hear her taking several small shuddering breaths, struggles to breathe.

PETER *(softly)*
Are you okay?

DIANA
I have to look out for myself
because you cannot.
You are not capable of looking
out for me anymore
Peter
And it feels *really* bad.
(pause)

I'm gonna move into Holly's
old room
Okay? So // just

PETER *(suddenly amped up)*
I'm tired too You're not the only one who's tired, but we have to finish this We're running out of room on the tape.

DIANA
This isn't about that.

PETER *(speaking quickly)*
You can't ask me to help you and not help you. I can't do both at the same time What are you asking for? You're always talking about communicating but I'm *trying* to communicate with you. *You're* the one who's bad at communicating. You *demand* my help. I don't *have* to do it.

DIANA
No Peter. You *do*. You *do* have to do it. And it's not good for either of us anymore. We have to stop. Okay?
(pause)
I think we need to just keep it professional.
(pause)
Okay?

PETER
You are so selfish and so freaking self-involved.

DIANA
Well so are you
but that's what it is.
(beat)
I'm gonna move into Holly's room tonight.
And we're gonna finish this vocal //

PETER
NO //

DIANA
And then I'll see you tomorrow and we'll have our coffee and we're gonna sing together on tour and it's gonna be great okay?
(pause)
It could have gone another way
but that's not what happened
it's just—that's not how it went and we need to accept it.

PETER
I don't accept it.

DIANA
You can't have your way Peter
Not with this.

Pause.

PETER *(numb)*
Okay.

DIANA
I'm gonna finish laying down
the vocals
And // then

PETER
Okay well Go fuck yourself.

Peter appears in the sound room and marches toward the control room.

Grover quickly shuts off talkback. Peter says a few more inaudible things as he enters control room. He sits back down in the producer's chair and puts on headphones and waits. There's an awkward moment Sound room is empty. Grover turns the sound on.

GROVER *(talkback)*
Whenever you're ready.

Diana enters, rattled. She drinks a bit of water.

DIANA
One second.

She clears her throat.

GROVER *(talkback)*
You need a break?

DIANA
Just give me a second.

Pause.
She walks resolutely to the headphones.

DIANA
Can we take the whole verse?

Grover signals to her.

DIANA
To the east of Eden
Flowers in my hair
Stumble from the garden
I didn't even care
Why do you still refuse me?
Kindness is crawling after you
Why do we have to choose when
Everything you got is right in front of you.

It is painful, more intense, note perfect.

GROVER *(to Peter)*
What do you think?

PETER *(quiet, still)*
Lock that one.

GROVER *(talkback)*
How'd that feel

DIANA
Good, I think.

GROVER *(talkback)*
Do you want to come in and have a listen?

Diana deliberates for a moment.

DIANA
Yeah.

She takes off her headphones, takes a breath, and then with resolve, walks into the control room.

Diana enters, makes the decision to stand next to Peter. Grover plays it back with the full instrumentation. They listen. He stops the tape.

GROVER
I think it sounds fucking great.

CHARLIE
Fucking amazing.

DIANA
Peter, what do you think?

Pause.

PETER
It's really good.

DIANA
Okay. *(beat)* Okay.

Diana starts to exit—then to Grover:

DIANA
Do you need me later?

GROVER
Maybe an hour?

DIANA
Okay
Just call me when it's time.

GROVER
Okay babe, go rest.

She exits through the kitchen.

PETER
That was good.

GROVER
Yeah.

Pause.

PETER
That was really good.

Silence.

2.

Peter, Charlie and Grover are listening to "Seven Roads."

Charlie brings up the faders and starts
playing what they have of a certain song.
Reg is sitting on the sofa in the
control room munching his salad.
He adds a bit of wheat germ.
They all sit and groove and listen to the
track together. They're having fun.

PETER
I wanna layer in a few more instruments
And I wanna change his bass to the alembic.

GROVER
But we still need to erase some old tracks
if you wanna layer in new stuff.

PETER
Okay.

GROVER
We could do two stereo background
tracks—or no, we could do three
mono tracks with two vocals a piece.

They listen some more.

PETER
My guitar sounds really basic
It's really stock.

GROVER
I haven't even done anything to it yet.

PETER
I have to do this over.

GROVER
You sure?

PETER
What?

GROVER
No man I just
I thought we locked that yesterday.

PETER
I don't like it.

GROVER *(forced)*
Okay.

PETER
I want to do it over
I brought my Les Paul in
I think it could be really good.
(he stands)
We can do it really quick.

GROVER
You seem kinda beat
You sure you don't wanna take a break?

PETER
No I wanna keep going
We'll do it in one take.
(starts to exit to the sound room)

Charlie stops the tape.

GROVER
Okay.

PETER
Actually, you know what?
I'm gonna go pee, I'll be right back.

Peter exits.
Once he's gone Charlie and Grover
have a moment.
Grover puts his finger to his lips.
He checks the mic to make sure they
aren't bugged.

GROVER
Fucking Watergate in here.
(he pulls him close)
Okay,

CHARLIE
What?

GROVER
So another turn of the screw:

CHARLIE
Uh-huh?

GROVER
Holly and Reg?
Splitsville.

CHARLIE
Are they done done? or //

GROVER
I was outside and Holly was crying
and she said this was a mistake I made
a huge mistake, and then Reg
started crying and he was all
you're bleeding me dry, you're bleeding me dry.
And then Holly was like *shut up shut up.*
And then she threw her ring on the ground
and then she started like screaming
my ring my ring. And then Reg
was all goddam you
Pick it up Pick it up! and
then Reg started crying
and then they were both just
crying and screaming.

CHARLIE
Jesus Christ.

GROVER.
I'm not trying to gossip but
we need to know these things
we need to have a strategy.

CHARLIE
Okay cool
What should we strategize?

Beat.

GROVER
I don't know I'm too tired
Peter kept me here all night.

CHARLIE
Serious?

GROVER
He just wants me me me—me all the time
He's like obsessed with me or something.
He always wants me to get stoned with him.
I can't work stoned all the time!

CHARLIE
So tell him.

GROVER
No man I can't
he gets really uncomfortable.
He gets weird with me.
Peter is a terror //

CHARLIE
I *know* //

GROVER
Peter is a fucking terror *No you don't know*!
Right after you left last night he was like oh hey
Grover can we just look at this for ten minutes—
and then ten minutes turned into literally
TEN HOURS.

CHARLIE
What?

GROVER
Yeah he changed his mind about
five hundred things.
Then he was like
"oh you know what change all that back"
—I'm all "oh great!" And the next thing I know
it's six in the morning
and he's like okay goodnight—I'm
like okay YOU CRAZY FUCK!
And just as I'm leaving the studio fucken
Simon bounces in all "*'ello matey! Ahoy ahoy!*"

CHARLIE
Oh shit

GROVER
I'm like *WHY* are you *HERE* It's *six* in
the fucken *MORNING*, go back to sleep! He's
like "I'm wound up with excitement Gotta
do me drums!"
And there's like seven hours of this
whole scenario with the drum—"oh" "Oh" "ah"

"there's a noise" "do you hear it"
"Do you hear it? Now? Now? NOW?"
And I'm like WHAT
THE FUCK IS WRONG WITH YOU?

CHARLIE
Jesus.

Grover puts his head down for a moment, exhausted.

GROVER
I'm okay. Just let me close my eyes.
I just need
to sleep at some point—but I took coke
so I'm up, but it's that shitty up you get
from coke.
I just need like three hours.
No like four hours
for sleep. Just like four hours
would be okay.
(beat)
We gotta do something.
We gotta start working in shifts—
you do 12 to 6 and I'll do 6 to 12 . . .

CHARLIE
So we'll work in shifts.

GROVER
We gotta figure something out
'cause I can't take this anymore.
We've been here almost a
fucken *year*.
I have a life.
I have a girlfriend.

CHARLIE
You do?

GROVER *(indignant)*
PAULA!

CHARLIE *(gingerly)*
You don't think she's kind of a user?

GROVER
What are you talking about?

CHARLIE
I don't know . . . I heard some stuff //

GROVER
I don't wanna *hear it* man.
(short pause)
I just want to sleep.
I want to close my eyes.

Charlie stares at him for a little while.
Grover—too out of it to be self-conscious—
stares back.

CHARLIE
Your eyes remind me of this painting
I once saw in France.
The painting was of a room of paintings
hung on a wall. It was cool.
The color of the wall was this
burning red color and that's the
color of your eyes.

GROVER
Where's the bag?

Charlie passes the cocaine bag to Grover.
Peter enters the control room.

PETER
Okay, wheels up!
(Grover pushes the bag aside)
I think this is gonna sound really good.

Peter enters the sound room, grabs his guitar, strums. He strums his guitar again.

Holly enters, sits, and lights a cigarette.

GROVER
Okay wheels up
You ready?

Charlie rewinds tape.

PETER
Yep.

GROVER
Where you wanna roll from?

PETER
Just right at the end of the second verse is good.

GROVER
Okay here we go . . .

Grover puts on the cans.
Charlie rewinds the tape.
Charlie rolls the tape.

Peter plays a bit, then stops.

Charlie stops the tape.

PETER *(inaudible)*
Let me take that one more time.

GROVER
You got it.

Charlie rewinds the tape.

Peter takes a contemplative beat.

Simon enters the control room, slumps next to Holly on the sofa. He's wearing a cape like a superhero.

Peter gives a thumbs-up sign, ready to go.

Charlie rolls the tape.

SIMON *(American accent)*
"Whatcha *doin'*?"
(beat)
"Whatcha *doin'*?"

Holly giggles, flips a page in her magazine.
Charlie stops the tape.

PETER *(inaudible)*
I don't think I can play all the way to the end—you need to punch me in later.

GROVER *(talkback)*
We have a ton of takes from yesterday
I can comp it together.

Peter moves the stool a little closer to the mic. Strums his guitar.

Charlie rewinds the tape.

PETER *(inaudible)*
Okay—I'm ready.

GROVER *(talkback)*
Okay here we go . . .

Charlie rolls the tape.

Peter starts to play the guitar part.

Over which Holly and Simon have a smoke and drink on the sofa in the control room.

HOLLY
You look knackered.

SIMON
I'm not terribly well.
Elyse is leaving me.

HOLLY
What?

Pause.

HOLLY
What happened?

SIMON
I don't want to get into it.

Pause.

HOLLY *(horrified)*
Oh Simon. God.

SIMON
She was going to come out to LA with
the kids but that's shot.
I just think they all hate me.
(he shakes his head in despair)
I need to see my fucking children
I can't be without them.

HOLLY
I know.

SIMON
No, you don't. You can't know.
Unless you have babies you can't know.
(pause)
Elyse I can almost take. *Almost.*
But I can't not have my kids. I can't.
I can't have them hate me.

Long pause.

HOLLY
You'll get back to London when we're done
and you can sort it all out then.

SIMON
How am I gonna sort it out?
And when am I gonna do that—
we were supposed to be in America
for six months Holly—six *months*!
And we haven't been back for *three years*!

Charlie stops the tape.

PETER *(inaudible)*
How was that?

GROVER *(talkback)*
I thought it was excellent
You want to have a listen?

Peter removes his guitar, bounces into the control room.

Charlie rewinds the tape.

PETER
Okay, let's hear.

Grover plays the track.
Peter listens for a few seconds.

PETER
You know what? Erase it.
(beat;
Charlie stops the tape)
I can do better. Let me have another go.

GROVER
Let's just hold on to that one.

PETER
We're running out of space
on the tape
Just record over it.

GROVER
Whatever you say.

Peter bounces back into the sound room.
Charlie rewinds the tape.

GROVER *(talkback)*
You ready?

PETER
Yep.

Charlie rolls the tape.

GROVER *(talkback)*
Okay, we're rolling.

Red lights blink on the console.

Peter starts playing—it's more elaborate than what he was doing before . . . he stops midway.

Charlie stops the tape.

PETER
That's wrong, huh.

GROVER *(talkback)*
I liked it simpler.

PETER
Yeah, me too.
Alright
Let's go back to the one I just did.

Grover and Charlie look at each other.

CHARLIE
Fuck.

GROVER *(talkback)*
We erased it.

PETER
What do you mean you erased it?

GROVER *(talkback)*
You just asked me to record over it.

PETER
Why the fuck would you do that?

GROVER *(talkback)*
You asked me to.

PETER
YOU FUCKING MORON
ARE YOU A FUCKING
IDIOT?
(pause)
WHAT THE FUCK IS
WRONG WITH YOUR
BRAIN?
HEY *FUCKFACE* I'M
TALKING TO YOU!

Peter throws off his headphones.

Peter storms into the control room, heads for Grover—

PETER
DO YOU WANT YOUR
NECK // BROKEN?

SIMON
Peter! //

Charlie gets up and intercedes—it gets crazy very quickly.

CHARLIE
Whoa! // WHOA!

PETER
YOU TWIT! WHAT THE
FUCK IS WRONG WITH
YOU?

IS SOMETHING // WRONG
WITH YOUR BRAIN?

GROVER
YOU TOLD ME TO
ERASE // THE TRACK

Peter marches at Grover, shoves him hard, advances, shoves him again.

CHARLIE
WHOA! PETER! // HEY HEY!

Simon rushes over and pulls Peter away.

SIMON
YOU TOLD HIM TO ERASE THE
BLOODY TRACK PETER.
(Peter starts to calm down)
Just do it over, man.

PETER *(to Grover)*
Fucking asshole.
You're fired. YOU'RE FIRED, GET THE
FUCK OUT OF HERE YOU'RE FIRED!

Peter slams his fist into the wall—exits. Grover is seriously rattled.

SIMON
You're not fired. He's just being a complete fucking asshole at the moment.

GROVER
He told me to record over it.

SIMON
You're alright. Why don't you have
a drink and we'll take a break.

Grover exits.

SIMON
Go have a drink with him.

Charlie nods, exits with Grover.
It's silent for a moment.
Simon and Holly just stand there
looking at one another in disbelief.

SIMON
What the bloody fuck?

Pause.

SIMON
Did you see that?
Peter nearly killed our engineer.
(pause)
What the bloody *fuck*!
He practically murdered Grover!

HOLLY
Poor Grover.

SIMON
Poor *Grover*? What about poor
Simon? Look at this—
(shows her his arm)

HOLLY
Oh my god!

Holly starts laughing.

SIMON
You think it's funny? Look at this!

HOLLY *(she checks out the arm)*
Oh my god You're bleeding.

SIMON
I need stitches from his—*pinky* fingernail,
Jesus Christ. He's like an alley cat.

She almost falls over screaming with laughter—
the laughter of exhaustion. Simon sucks on
the wound a little and stares at it.

SIMON
Why are you laughing?
He's like a rabid animal.

Her laughter is contagious and suddenly
they are both laughing from the insanity
of the whole thing. This goes on for a bit.

After it subsides:

SIMON
I dunno what we're gonna do. He's absolutely
brilliant, but god is Peter a fucking *nightmare*.

HOLLY *(wiping tears of laughter)*
I'm sorry darling, do you want a hug?

SIMON
Of *course* I want a bloody hug,
what the hell is wrong with you?

She extends her arms—she's being the mummy.

HOLLY
There there.

SIMON
I never thought I'd be the sort of person
who said things like "I miss the old days"
but I do. I miss when it was just the three of us,
and we all got on
and played our little concerts
and drank our pints at the pub
and had holidays at Mykonos
and sat on the beach and got pissed.

She gives him a peck on the lips.

HOLLY
Your beard smells like pot.
And vomit.

SIMON
Well I've been smoking pot and vomiting Can
you blame me?

This makes them both laugh.

3.

They all listen as a group to a newly completed mix of "Seven Roads," including a brilliant guitar solo that Grover has made out of pieces from the previous scene. Diana sits as far from Peter as she can without making a spectacle of herself.

PETER
You're a genius.

GROVER
I just comped it together from a few takes.

PETER
It's seamless
It's—I'm not gonna say flawless
But
Wow.

GROVER
I still want to layer in a few more tracks.

PETER
Oh we're nowhere near done
But it's a great start.

Beat.

GROVER *(politic but dying inside)*
Good.
(beat)
Should we break for dinner?

SIMON
What time is it?

CHARLIE
8:15.

SIMON
Okay let's break.

Charlie stops the tape.
The group disperses.
Reg exits into the kitchen as
Diana approaches Simon.

DIANA *(to Simon)*
My tambourine sounds really thin
I have to do it over //

SIMON
So we'll do // it over

DIANA
It sounds like I'm playing with my //
sister's bracelets.

CHARLIE
Did everyone put their order in?

He waves the menu around.
Everyone ignores him.
He folds the menu and sticks it in his back pocket.

Diana exits the studio.

Simon hops on the couch, lies down with
a magazine and eventually falls asleep.

Holly curls up with Simon, puts a coat over
her and takes a slight nap.
Peter approaches Grover and Charlie
near the console.

PETER
I'm sorry about the other day.
I was an asshole.
You were just doing your job.

GROVER
It's okay, man. No sweat.

PETER *(to Charlie)*
Sorry man.

CHARLIE
I'm sorry too.
I mean for you.

Uncomfortable beat. Then Peter and Charlie hug it out—but awkward. Peter hugs Grover, also awkward.

PETER
Come out to Agatha's tonight, okay?

GROVER
Okay.

CHARLIE
Okay.

PETER
Not you, I meant Grover.

CHARLIE
Oh.

PETER
KIDDING! Of course you!

Peter exits the studio.

CHARLIE
That was cool of him.

GROVER
He's an asshole.
I hate Peter.

CHARLIE
You're a good actor.

GROVER
I'm a politician.
I'm a shrink I'm a politician
It's all politics, man
everyone's fucking insane.

CHARLIE
The inmates are running the asylum //

GROVER
He steals my weed //

CHARLIE *(finishing his thought)*
Just like in Vonnegut //

GROVER *(finishing his thought)*
I don't give a shit
I don't want to waste my energy
on psychopaths.
I just want to get my Grammy
and never see his face again.

CHARLIE
Dude
You are stone cold.

GROVER
Because I learned.
If you don't learn you suffer.
My dad walked out when I was a kid and
that's what my mom told me:
Suffer and Learn.
So I learned.

Charlie looks over at him.
Reg enters, approaches Grover and Charlie.

REG
How do you lads feel about switching
studios?

CHARLIE
I'm looking forward to it.
I like LA.

REG
I love it.

CHARLIE
Oh yeah?

REG
I love LA.
Nature
The howling canyons and chasms
Palm trees
It's my speed.
(beat)
Paula and I are moving in together.

Grover's face freezes in horror.
Charlie looks to Grover with sympathy.

REG
I found us a house in the Hollywood Hills
Very cozy Simon's taking the upstairs floor.
So It'll be the three of us
my best mate, Paula and myself.

Grover is still a mask of frozen horror.

CHARLIE
That's nice.

REG
I want to be around people who I love
and who love me.
(beat)
You can give up on a person but you
can't ever, ever give up on love.
Not love itself.
(moved—slightly grievous)
Not ever.
(suddenly too intense)
EVER.

It gets pretty heavy.
Then:

CHARLIE
I'm gonna go put the order in.
(he sees sad Grover)
Or we could pick up the order together.
You wanna come with me?

GROVER
No. I'm fine.

Grover sits at the console and begins to roll a joint.

Charlie exits the studio.

Holly has been observing the whole scene, dragging on her cigarette. She's like a block of ice.

HOLLY *(to Reg)*
I'm happy for you, I'm not bothered.
I want you to bring her 'round.

You can shag her right there on the
console if you like Is that what you want?

She puts out her cigarette.
Reg approaches Holly tentatively.

REG
I want you to be happy
I wasn't a good husband to you
I'm sorry I made you so miserable
It was never my intention
You were a wonderful wife to me
And you deserve happiness.

Holly looks at him for a good long while.

HOLLY
You think you can just dispose of people
like trash?
(glaring at him)
If I'm so wonderful
why have you disposed of me like
fucking rubbish?

REG
You broke up with *me*.
You don't want to be with me

HOLLY
No no no I don't want to hear *this*
(she makes a talking face with her hand)
Tell me something I want to hear
Not some stock phrase out of a book.

REG *(totally confused)*
What?

Holly looks at him, then breaks out
in quiet laughter.

HOLLY *(as if he's just proved her point)*
You see?

REG
Look
I've come to you with goodwill.

HOLLY
Yes, very goodwill. Thank you.
Thanks for that Reg. For your goodwill.

REG
You're being unreasonable

HOLLY
I don't bloody care if I *am* being unreasonable

REG *(exasperated)*
You *left* me //

HOLLY
And don't you dare tell me what I deserve:
I don't *deserve* happiness
No one *deserves*
anything
You don't *get* what you deserve
in this life.
You don't know a thing *about* life—

She is suddenly filled with overwhelming sadness.

He goes to touch her, she flinches.
She stands for a moment looking away from him,

goes to the console.
She pours herself another glass of champagne,
ignores him.
He watches her and walks away.

She stands for a moment, unsmiling.
She looks over at Grover rolling the joint—
changes her mood very suddenly.

HOLLY
God that *spliff* is—
is that for me?

GROVER *(cheeky)*
Roll your own.

HOLLY
That's that stuff from Santa Cruz?
(Grover starts laughing)
Oh my god
you know Grover you have to share
don't be stingy.

GROVER
I'm not stingy You're the one who's stingy.

They both start laughing at some
private joke.

HOLLY
Are you gonna bring that up again?

GROVER
Nah.

HOLLY
What are you doing after rehearsal tonight?

GROVER
Oh man, I'm beat
I think I'm just gonna watch television
and get baked.

HOLLY
Do you know what's playing at the
revival theater? *Don't Look Now.*

GROVER
What is that?

HOLLY
You don't know it?
It's // got that

GROVER
Unh-uh.

HOLLY
Oh my God
It's one of the most erotic scenes in
all of cinema. I mean to // me, it's

GROVER
I don't know it //

Grover lights the joint and takes a toke,
then passes it to Holly over the following.
They pass it back and forth.

HOLLY
It's just extraordinary.

GROVER
Don't know it but
What about *Last Tango*.

HOLLY
Now see I didn't find that particularly
erotic.

GROVER
What?

HOLLY
But I'm not a fan of Marlon
Brando // whereas

GROVER
You're crazy.

HOLLY
No, well,

GROVER
Brando.

HOLLY
Not my taste.

GROVER
Brando isn't your taste.

HOLLY
Marlon Brando is very sexy but in a—
well here's the // thing about Brando here's

GROVER
Tell me.

HOLLY
the thing about him: you see
Marlon Brando means to debase
all the women he loves and
that has never appealed to me.

GROVER
Every chick I ever met, every last one
has wanted to make it with Brando.

HOLLY
Not // me

GROVER
Every last one.

HOLLY
I feel just the opposite, I don't fancy him.
I think he's selfish and mean.

GROVER
You know him?

HOLLY
I know Donald Sutherland.

GROVER
Personally?

HOLLY *(innocent)*
No.

Beat.

GROVER
You're— *(he cracks up)*

HOLLY
Now wait a minute wait a // minute

GROVER
No //

HOLLY
No come on //

GROVER
No You don't have any credibility.

HOLLY
Why?

GROVER
Because you make shit up!

HOLLY *(laughing at herself)*
I have all sorts of credibility
My mother was a—primary school teacher
I'm credible.

GROVER
This isn't about your // mother

HOLLY
Here's the thing
She's—I like my mother—but
Here's the thing Donald Sutherland
alright
is very sensual
very ordinary And you can see he's very
uh
befuddled he's // got those

GROVER
Befuddled.

HOLLY
Yeah he's—

GROVER
What's that mean—

HOLLY
Befuddled, you know
he's got suede patches on his jackets.
You know
but he's also quite confident
and that to me is potent that mix.

GROVER
Befuddled and ordinary?
That's what you like?

HOLLY
Well
Yeah.

GROVER
That's like the garbage man!

HOLLY
So what's wrong with the garbage man?
Don't be a snob Grover,

GROVER
I'm not a snob.

HOLLY
Well I don't know
I think it takes a certain lack of ego to
be a garbage man
to clean up other people's messes, that's an
incredible thing, to give of yourself
and tarry in the muck
and ask for so little from the world.
I can find a way to make myself useful
to that sort of man
whereas with Marlon Brando
I think I'd be inclined to you know
smear myself with
with crap or
mud or something because he doesn't
like women.

GROVER
I like women.

HOLLY
I mean as people.

GROVER
Yeah—people! that's what I like!

HOLLY *(flirting a little)*
I don't believe you.

GROVER
Why would I //

HOLLY
Because you're always playing with
your knobs.

She cracks herself up.

GROVER
Huh?

HOLLY
Gimme that *(he passes, she tokes)*
So who are you seeing Grover, are // you

GROVER
Okay so I'm a snob and I'm a liar—

HOLLY
No-no—Grover no It's not your fault it's
the fault of your sex
if you think of it.
For example peacocks
I saw something on telly where boy peacocks
only know who to shag because of the gleam
of the feathers from a girl peacock.
It's a swirl of color.
That's all we are to you
we're things in poses;
we're, you know, shapes
things you can squish and sink into.

GROVER
First of all that's bullshit.

HOLLY
No it isn't.

GROVER
It's *bullshit*.

HOLLY
Okay.

GROVER
And I'm not talking about the squishing
thing I'm talking about
the peacocks.
'Cause peacocks and I don't know a shit ton
about peacocks
But peacocks All peacocks have color
Every peacock has iridescent
what's it called?

HOLLY
Oh yeah //

GROVER
That's why peacocks //

HOLLY
Oh you're right.

GROVER
Right?

HOLLY
Why did I // think—?

GROVER
I *am* right //

HOLLY
Well never mind.
But the principle remains
I still believe in the principle
There's a
A blindness you men have.

GROVER
What about you?

HOLLY
Us women?

GROVER
No: *you*
You Personally.

Beat.

HOLLY
Grover don't flirt.

GROVER
I'm not flirting.

Pause.

HOLLY
Are you seeing someone?

Grover's smile fades.

GROVER
Yeah. I am.

HOLLY
Are you?

GROVER
Gina.

HOLLY
The girl who brings us the paper napkins?
The girl with the yellow jumper?

GROVER
Yeah.

HOLLY
That Gina?

GROVER
Yeah.

HOLLY
Are you dating?

GROVER
Oh come on.

HOLLY
Are you shagging?

GROVER
Not yet
It's still
No
Not yet
But it's on
It's on okay? it's happening.

HOLLY
I believe you.

GROVER
Believe me.

Pause.

HOLLY *(looks him in the eye)*
Have you ever been in love?

Beat.

GROVER
Me?

HOLLY
You have to be careful Grover;
it's dangerous to trust people.
It's dangerous for your heart.

Holly's facade is starting to crack.
She takes a puff of the joint, forces a tiny smile.

HOLLY
Anyway you have to see *Don't Look Now*.

GROVER
I will.

HOLLY
It is an erotic
Epiphany
I mean experience
Don't Look Now.

GROVER
I'll look out for it.

Simon wakes up from his nap, sits up.

HOLLY
The scene where Julie Christie and Donald
make love is so passionate, so felt—and
he shoots it on a split screen.

GROVER *(scandalized)*
Shoots what?

HOLLY
No, the *director*.

GROVER
Oh.

HOLLY
So you see it while they're fucking
and then the aftermath simultaneously.

SIMON
I dig that Julie Christie.

HOLLY *(to Simon)*
Do you fancy her?

Simon stands up and starts making out with himself.

HOLLY
You fancy her.

Simon starts licking the Neve board.

HOLLY *(to Simon)*
Did you see it? *Don't Look Now*?

SIMON
It was the most erotic adult film experience
of my adult life.

HOLLY
Isn't it?

SIMON
I took Elyse to see it and after we walked out
she said, well I've just lost weight
seeing that.

HOLLY
Did she hate it?

SIMON
She *loved* it
An' I'll tell you something
I'll tell you something else
Julie Christie's buttocks
are like two
scoops of ice cream.

HOLLY
And there's this other scene that I found
really wild which was the scene—

SIMON *(tokes from the joint)*
With the dwarf?

HOLLY
No but that was incredibly // frightening

SIMON
The hooded dwarf!

HOLLY
Let me finish, you never let me speak.
It's the scene in the restaurant

with the two women remember?
and one is a fortune teller and she's
really weird and sort of unattractive
and they—remember this scene?
(watching it on the screen of her mind)
And she grabs on to the tablecloth
in the restaurant and she's
for some reason she passes out,
it's preternatural
and it happens in slow motion
she clasps on to the tablecloth and
she's passing out
and the dishes and cutlery and
everything comes
crashing to the floor
smashing and breaking there's
glass everywhere.
and she passes out
and they take her
the crazy fortune teller and the
old woman with cataracts
they take her to the WC
and the fortune teller starts telling her
her fortune
about her daughter
a daughter that died
her young daughter . . .
and, uh . . .

Holly cuts herself off,
suddenly overcome with emotion.

GROVER
That's sad.

HOLLY
It is sad
(pause)
Maybe that's why the sex scene is so beautiful.
because you know it's coming from grief.
Because the grief is
tearing the couple apart
but then it's bringing them together
at the same time.
(beat)
In this very strange way.

ACT IV

GOODBYE YELLOW BRICK ROAD

1.

We are in a new studio in Los Angeles.

Diana, Holly and Peter are overdubbing a harmony section together. They share a single microphone, uncomfortably close; Holly in the middle. They sound ethereal, almost otherworldly.

DIANA, PETER AND HOLLY

Just call me when
Ooh
Just call me when
Ooh
Just call me when

Ooh
Ooh

We can see Grover and Charlie's heads rocking with the music, so into it.

Diana is wearing dark sunglasses. Everyone looks more polished or glammed out, almost as though they traversed the bumps of the middle seventies in the break.

When they finish the harmonies, Charlie stops and rewinds the tape.

GROVER *(talkback)*
That was fucking *beautiful*
let's double it.

CHARLIE *(to Grover)*
I think one of the channels
just went.

GROVER
Huh?

HOLLY
Are we done?

GROVER *(talkback)*
Hold on a minute
(to Charlie)
Which?

CHARLIE
Bad EQ on channel 10.

Grover has a look—

GROVER
Aw fuck.
(on talkback)
I'm sorry guys, the channel's dead.
Give us a sec?

Charlie repatches the cable.

Meanwhile the band members just stand around. Diana has a sip of Courvoisier.

GROVER *(hearing something)*
What's that?

CHARLIE
What?

GROVER
There's a ground hum, listen.

CHARLIE
Oh yeah.

GROVER
Unplug it.
I thought that channel was good.
(beat)
Try another patch cable? //

Charlie repatches the cable.

DIANA
I had mai tais with Tony Orlando last night . . .

HOLLY
You're kidding.

DIANA
Unh-uh. He was at Wang Fu.

HOLLY
He's so // sexy

CHARLIE
It's still there.

GROVER
Shit. Unplug it?

CHARLIE
I'll call down to the shop.

Charlie picks up the phone and dials.

HOLLY
Was Dawn there?

DIANA
I don't think they hang out
at all.
Just professional.

HOLLY
I thought they were shagging.

GROVER
Is anyone even // there?

DIANA
That was not my
understanding.
At all.
He was // flirting like crazy

GROVER
What time is it?

CHARLIE
Four.

HOLLY
Was he.

Diana nods.

GROVER
In the *morning*?

CHARLIE
Yeah.

GROVER
We gotta go back to working
in shifts
(talkback)
I'm sorry bear with us.

Pause.

HOLLY
Sad for Dawn.

CHARLIE *(into phone)*
It's Charlie over in 4.
Good.
Um, we have a problem with
one of the modules.
Yeah, so the channel died and
we patched around it,
but there's a ground hum.
Do you guys have another
channel?
Okay thanks.

He waits.

GROVER
Is that Tammy?

Charlie shrugs.

GROVER
I wanted to tell her //
something.

DIANA
Always darkest before the
Dawn.

Holly laughs quietly about this—they're kind of slaphappy. Holly makes Diana giggle. Peter is stone-faced. The more they laugh the more he hates it.

DIANA
It's really not that funny.

HOLLY
Yeah
I thought about it the other
day and I thought
Wow, I'm really humorless.

DIANA
That's what you thought
about?

HOLLY
Yeah.

This makes Diana bust up noiselessly. They both giggle/snort quietly over the mics. They look over at one another, but of course there's funereal Peter like a Greek Column to the right.

CHARLIE *(to Grover)*
There's no extra channel.
(into phone)
Okay, thanks.

He hangs up the phone.
Grover's heart sinks.

GROVER
What do we do?

CHARLIE
I don't know.

HOLLY *(to herself)*
Why am I stuck to the floor?

DIANA
Someone spilled a bottle of
Jack Daniel's all over the carpet.

HOLLY
Look
I'm literally glued in place here.

She tries to move around—kind of falls on Diana. She giggles. Diana giggles.

PETER
Could you stop *talking*? //

DIANA *(whips over to stare him down)*
SHUT YOUR GODDAM MOUTH.

Everyone in the studio kind of freezes—all bracing for something.

Hideous awful silence.

CHARLIE *(silently panicking)*
What if we like move the fader up and down?

GROVER
What?

CHARLIE
Yeah like maybe there's dust in the fader.
That's happened to me before—and we could smooth it out!

GROVER
Try it.

Charlie moves the fader up and down, there's still a ground hum.

GROVER
That's not doing anything.

CHARLIE
Hold on.

He moves the fader up and down manically.

GROVER
You're gonna break it!

Grover pulls Charlie away from he fader, covers his face with his hands.

CHARLIE
Maybe we should just
let them go and
we'll do it tomorrow.

GROVER
Are you *fucking* kidding me?
How are we going to get
these people
together in the same room
again?
Like *ever*?

They stew in tormented silence.

GROVER
What if we blow some
compressed air on it?
Let's get the screws out.

Charlie looks for the tool kit.

DIANA *(determined not to be silenced)*
How was St. Thomas?

Holly darts her eyes around nervously—she's scared to say anything.

HOLLY *(extremely quiet)*
Good.

Pause.

DIANA
You can talk.

HOLLY *(tiny)*
I know //

PETER
Don't ever
Fucking tell *me* to shut up //
ever

Diana shakes her head and chuckles to herself.

DIANA
You are so sad and // pathetic
Do you know that?

PETER
Oh *I'm* // sad okay

DIANA
You just told us to shut up and now you're
telling *me*
not to tell you to // *shut up*?

PETER
You're giving me a
FUCKING HEADACHE.

Pause.

HOLLY *(to control room)*
Hello? Anyone out there?

GROVER *(talkback)*
Give us another minute
Sorry guys.

Grover throws the tool kit open, hurriedly pulls out the screwdriver and starts taking out the screws in the module as Charlie looks on.

DIANA *(to herself)*
He's sorry . . .
(laughs, shakes head, sighs)

Long pause.

DIANA *(to Holly)*
So what were you saying?

Pause.

HOLLY
Huh?

DIANA
What were you saying before?

HOLLY
I didn't say anything.

Pause.

DIANA
Don't let him silence you.
Say anything you want.

Beat.

HOLLY
Okay.

DIANA
It's fine.

Pause.

HOLLY *(quiet)*
I just wasn't saying anything.

Holly drinks some champagne nervously. Diana pulls a vial of coke out from her boot. She does a line on the back of her hand.

DIANA
Tony Orlando was totally coming on to me.
(pause)
He gave me his number.

PETER *(under his breath)*
Slut.

DIANA
What?
What was // that?

CHARLIE *(to Grover, quietly)*
Hurry up.

GROVER *(under his breath)*
I'm hurrying
Help me, fuckface!

Charlie blows compressed air onto the unscrewed module. They re-screw the channel back in.

DIANA
I heard you.
I heard you motherfucker //

PETER
SHUT UP AND DO //
THE TRACK

DIANA
You MOTHERFUCKER

PETER
DO THE TRACK

DIANA
GO // TO HELL

PETER
DO THE *FUCKING* TRACK
DO THE TRACK
STOP WASTING
EVERYONE'S TIME //
WITH

DIANA
Don't tell me // to *shut up*

PETER
YOUR PRIMA DONNA
BULLSHIT.

DIANA
How *dare* you!
(pause)
I am a *lady*.

Charlie gives him the thumbs-up.

PETER
You know what //

DIANA
NO, DO // *YOU* KNOW WHAT!

PETER
Do you even care that you're wasting everyone's time with this solipsistic // nonsense?

GROVER *(talkback)*
Okay we're // back

PETER
YOU *INFANT*?
DO YOU CARE? *AT ALL?*

Diana shuts her eyes and takes a calming breath.

GROVER *(talkback)*
We're back //

PETER
I think you need to stop snorting so much coke It's going to your brain.

Holly pours herself some champagne and then downs half a bottle.

DIANA *(to Grover)*
Just play the track. Let's go.

GROVER
You ready // ?

DIANA *(to Peter, almost a spasm)*
Do you know
I can't stand to look at your
face
I can't stand to hear your //
voice

PETER
Goddam you!!!!!

DIANA
GET OUT OF MY LIFE
I DON'T WANT YOU IN //
MY LIFE

PETER
I'M NOT IN YOUR LIFE!!!

Short pause.

DIANA
I am physically repulsed by
you Do you know that?
My skin is crawling
I can't stand being near you.

PETER
Do you want me to break
your neck?
Maybe then you could stand it
'cause you'd be paralyzed.

DIANA
Oh you're gonna break my neck?
(to Holly)
Did you hear that? You hear what he—
(to Peter)
YOU'RE GONNA BREAK MY NECK IN FRONT OF GROVER AND HOLLY AND—AND
(not remembering Charlie's name)
AND EVERYONE?! YOU'RE GONNA BREAK MY NECK? NO PETER *I DON'T THINK SO*!

Dead silence.

GROVER
Let's
No one break anyone's neck and let's lay one down.
Channel's fixed
Let's do this and everyone can get out of // here

DIANA *(under her breath)*
Coward.

PETER
I should burn your hair off.

DIANA
What?

PETER
I should burn your hair off
I'd like to see you bald.

DIANA
Yeah you do that
Asshole.

HOLLY
Grover, what are we doing
standing here all night?
Why are you *stranding* us?

GROVER
I've been ready to go.

HOLLY
THEN SAY SOMETHING!
DON'T JUST SIT BEHIND
YOUR SMUG LITTLE
CONSOLE!

GROVER *(losing it)*
I SAID LET'S
LAY ONE DOWN
GODDAM YOU! I SAID IT
A HUNDRED TIMES
THE CHANNEL'S FIXED
WE *RE-FUCKING-PATCHED*
IT GODDAM YOU!

Pause.

HOLLY *(very professional)*
Okay, that's all I wanted to
know. Don't get so upset.

GROVER *(not sorry)*
Sorry.

PETER
That's okay man.

DIANA
Just
Let's just keep going.

Beat.

PETER *(quietly, to Diana)*
As little vibrato as possible //

DIANA *(calm)*
Shut the hell up.

GROVER
Waiting for speed . . .

Charlie rolls the tape.

DIANA, PETER AND HOLLY
Just call me when
Ooh
Just call me when
Ooh
Just call me when
Ooh
Ooh

Charlie stops the tape.
Nobody moves.
You could hear a pin drop.

2.

Peter, Charlie and Grover mixing "Domino."
Grover is playing with the faders—
pulling out tracks and isolating others.

GROVER
It doesn't all work together.
Everything is good but
it's clashing.
Here listen:

They listen.

PETER *(sighs)*
We need to do something about
the bass part.

GROVER *(checks his watch)*
He'll be here for the meeting.

PETER
Pull out the drums.

Charlie does. They listen some more.

PETER
Let me just hear the bass?

They listen.

PETER *(spazzing)*
FUUUUUUCK!

Charlie shuts off the tape.

GROVER
What don't you like about it? That // it's

PETER *(apes Reg's playing)*
It's all over the place man.

GROVER
I know what you mean.

PETER
I don't know how many times
I can say it to him. It's like stop showing
off *we get it, you're a virtuoso.*
(beat)
This happened in my last band.
(beat)
Hold on.
(he grabs a cassette, pops it in the player)
Here:

It's the bass part, but it's different.
He and Grover listen.

PETER
See how clean it is?
It gives the goddam whole song a *spine*.
That's what we were missing I'd
be happy just using this.

Reg walks in with Simon.

SIMON
Hello lads.

REG
Hello mates.

Upon seeing Reg, Grover shuts the tape off.

GROVER
Hi boys.

REG
What was that?

PETER
Well—you know
I just made a tape . . . to show you kind of
what I meant
About the bass part.

Beat.

REG
Okay.

PETER
Because it's still a little too ornamented.

REG
Yeah
It's too ornamented sure
So you want me to . . .

Beat.

PETER
What you did is good Reg //

REG
Right.

PETER
But it's still a little too swingy
You know?

Pause.

REG
You recorded that?

PETER
Yeah
Just to show you.

REG
Why don't you use that one?

Beat.

PETER
If you don't have a problem with that
Then great.

REG
Makes my life easy.

PETER
Okay.

REG
Maybe you don't need a bass player
on this album since
you play all the instruments.
You know what you want Peter.
(Beat. Reg checks his watch)
I'll be back for the meeting.

Reg leaves.

PETER *(to Simon)*
So what do you think? It's better, right?

Simon stares at him.

SIMON
Grover, can you give us a minute?

GROVER
Yeah sure.

Grover exits with Charlie.
Simon pours himself a glass of scotch.

SIMON *(as he pours)*
You know, I've known Reggie for many years.
Many many years.
You don't know Reg the way I know him;
I know there's this tension between you two
But you don't always understand where
Reg is coming from. I do.
I've known him a long
long time.

(he sips his drink;
Peter looks at him)
Look
Peter may I be candid?
You manipulated your way to
being the producer of this record.

PETER *(laughing in disbelief)*
You— // *what?*

SIMON
I'm not saying you don't deserve it
and I'm not saying you're not talented
you have tremendous vision
you did a brilliant job with the last album
and we have a number-one album.
But sometimes you can take it too far.
(beat)
It upsets me if you are recording
things at home.
It upsets me that you are
bringing in my parts and
Reggie's parts and asking
us to duplicate // your work

PETER
Yeah but I'm // not

SIMON
I give space to it and I respect it
but I'm not going to
have a conversation and pretend
it's all innocuous because it isn't.
So that's it.

PETER
But you admit I did a good job with
the last album.

SIMON
I love the album.
Mostly.
But it's the decision to *lay down*
for you that I *didn't* love.
I have trouble with that
I really do
I have trouble with that
and clearly Reg does too and
I don't blame him.
(beat)
You see Peter, here's the thing:
Not everything is going to be what *you* want.
Music isn't supposed to be perfect
It's not about that.
It's about relating to each other;
and making something *from your soul.*
And you are going to fall short;

PETER
My standards are // very high

SIMON
And you have to live with it //

PETER
I won't apologize to you for that
And I *do not fall short.*

SIMON
We all fall // short

PETER
Maybe you're accustomed to failure
Maybe before I got here you
let yourself off the hook
But I demand *excellence* from
myself and from everyone.
I raised the bar
and I make everyone better
and that's not boasting it's just true.
When we're done with
this process you will kiss my hand
and thank me.

A tiny smile on Simon's face.

SIMON
I love you Peter
but you're not a team player
and that's pretty clear.
You're the one throwing // your
toys around

PETER
I'm making the album better //

SIMON
You're going to need to compromise
or we're not gonna last.

PETER
It's a fine line between compromise
and losing yourself
I don't want to—
If I have an instinct I can't suppress it.

SIMON
I'm very sensitive to the nuances
of the songs too
Reg is creative
Just like you
I'm rather creative myself you see so
I don't like to always be told
No No No

PETER
But that's not // what I'm

SIMON
And I see your points sometimes
I do
but other times I feel you're just
being too *pushy*.
It's too much.
I mean that with respect
But it's *my band*.

PETER
It's not yours
It's *ours* //

SIMON
Well it certainly isn't *yours*
We aren't day players who
come in when you // need us and

PETER
Don't grab the aces like that //

SIMON
leave when it suits you

PETER
"I own the band"—NO
you can't say that
no
no // way

SIMON
Okay //

PETER *(deeply hurt)*
You can't say that to me
not after the past three years No way.

SIMON
You're right.

Short pause.

PETER *(quietly)*
I am killing myself for this record
Why can't you acknowledge how
hard I'm working?

SIMON *(not yielding)*
You seem upset, Peter.

PETER *(increasingly hurt)*
Why are you *speaking* to me like this?
Why do you want to hurt me?

SIMON
We're just having a conversation.

PETER
No This isn't how you are with Reg This
isn't how you are with
the rest of them It's *me*.

It's *just* me.
And I don't know what to do.
It's like the harder I work the
more you hate me.
The more I give to this band the more you
hate me I don't know what to do to stop
making you HATE ME!

Pause.

SIMON
I think we need to keep this
professional, Peter.

PETER
Oh right—you're a *professional*!
You're holding it all together.
'Cause you're the daddy right?
You're the *big man*?
(beat)
Well if you're such a great dad
where are your kids?
WHERE *IS* EVERYONE?

Simon looks at him for a moment; an iceberg.

SIMON
I'll see you at the meeting.

Simon starts to leave, Peter blocks him.

PETER
I have every reason in the world to
walk away
I have every reason to quit this band
and walk away from this.

SIMON
I'm relatively useless without
the band to play with.
It may be a form of insecurity.
But you'd do very well as a solo artist.
(beat)
You should do what feels
right for you Peter.
(pause)
I'm not going to keep doing triage
to make the wound heal.
Maybe it *won't* heal.
(beat)
Some wounds stay open.
That's alright.
*(drinks the remainder of his drink
and puts the glass down)*
It's alright.

Simon exits.

*Diana enters. She sees Peter and
turns to leave—*

PETER *(impulsively)*
Don't go.

Diana stops.

Long pause.

DIANA
Are we *talking* right now?

PETER
I don't know.
I think we are.

Pause.

DIANA
Where is everyone?
I thought there was a meeting.

Beat.

DIANA
What just happened in here?

A long pause. Peter quite suddenly breaks down sobbing.
He's falling apart in front of her.

DIANA
You're just tired baby
That's all.

Peter nods his head, then quietly:

PETER
Yeah.

DIANA
We've all been there.

PETER
I'm not a monster.

DIANA
No you're not.

PETER *(momentary stubbornness)*
I won't keep apologizing for
producing this album!

Pause.

PETER *(quiet, tender)*
I miss you
so much.

Pause.

PETER *(intensely vulnerable)*
I miss you.

Pause.

DIANA
I'm here fourteen hours a day Peter
I'm here all the // time

PETER
That's not what I mean.
I don't want you seeing other guys.

DIANA
Peter //

PETER
I can't work.
I can't function the way I *need* to
with you seeing other men.

DIANA
You can't tell me what to do.

She turns to go.

PETER
I'm sorry
Don't leave—*don't leave.*

Long pause.

DIANA
You *have* a girlfriend.

PETER
She's not my *family*
She's not my *heart*, you are.
You are.
You.

Diana takes off her sunglasses.
Her hand is shaking. Her eyes are all red.
She holds his hand. He kisses her hand.

PETER *(totally raw)*
I don't have a family
And I'll never have that You were right.
You were right about my father
I don't have close relationships
I'm not capable of it.
I'm alone.
(beat)
I am controlling because I am fearful
of losing everything
(then despairing, voice shuddering)
but it's happening no matter what I do.

DIANA
I can't take care of you.

PETER
Say you're my family.
SAY IT.

Pause.

DIANA *(getting pulled deep into it)*
Where is everyone.

He pulls her to him.
Very close. It's very intense.

PETER
Say it.
Say you're my family.
(beat)
SAY IT!

She looks at him,
She feels it's true—she wants to say it.
She loosens his grip.
She briskly exits the studio.

Peter is very still. Then he nods,
like he's resolved something in his mind.
He takes a breath.
Grover enters.

GROVER
Pssssst.
(Peter musters a tiny smile—Grover co-opted
his "psst" shtick)
Is the coast clear?

PETER
Is the coast *ever* clear? *Ever?*
(they laugh a little)
I would love a clear coast.

GROVER
There's food in the kitchen
why don't you get something
to eat?

Pause.

PETER
Yeah brother
Okay.
Yeah.

Peter exits through the sound room into the kitchen.

Reg enters the control room.

REG
Congratulations Grover
Sorry I couldn't be at the party.

GROVER
That's okay.

REG
Is this your first producing
credit?

GROVER
Yep.

REG
Well you earned it. You did.

Hugs him.

GROVER
Thank you Reggie
That means a lot.

REG
Are you happy?

GROVER *(smiling)*
Uhhh
I don't know if I'd go that far.

REG
Why not?

GROVER
I just
You know—I don't want to get complacent
I want to keep focused on my work.

REG
Why?

GROVER
Because I want to get better.

Beat.

REG
Why do you want to get better?

Beat.

GROVER *(a little uncomfortable)*
Because I want to do a good job man
I mean *(laughs)*
What are you driving at?

REG *(very serious)*
Why do you want to do a good job?

GROVER
Because . . . otherwise I'll
get in trouble?

REG
And if you get in trouble?

GROVER
I won't get to the next thing I need to do.

REG
But see I just think it's so American
this whole obsession with the
Next Thing.
Where are you *now*?
You should enjoy life.
You just had a good thing happen Grover
You got promoted to being a producer with Peter
On this album
You should be able to enjoy that.

GROVER *(taut smile)*
I'm not that guy.

REG
What guy?

GROVER
I guess I don't like to waste my time
I want to keep it moving.

REG
But
life is for enjoyment.

Grover laughs, like it's a joke.

GROVER
What are you talking about man?

REG *(serious)*
Don't laugh at me.

Pause.

GROVER
I'm sorry man I just
I guess I don't believe that.

REG
Then what do you believe?

Beat.

GROVER
Why is this getting all heavy?

REG
What do you believe Grover?

GROVER
I mean
I guess I believe we're here to suffer.

REG
You suffer if you choose to suffer
It's a choice.

GROVER *(slightly offended)*
Oh yeah?

REG
Or you can choose joy.

GROVER
No one's immune from suffering, Reg
That's just the human condition.

REG *(gently)*
But don't you // think

GROVER
There's joy
in bits and pieces, yeah
I've felt that, I know what happiness
feels like.
(beat)
But there's some
shit lesson life wants you to learn
only no one tells you what it is
or why you have to do it
You just have to muddle through
and make the best of it.
But life is pain
And people are disappointing
And that's why I like to work
And to get to the next thing.

REG
That's such a sad way to see life.

GROVER *(checks his watch)*
We got to have this meeting.

REG *(feeling lost)*
What about love?

GROVER
I don't want to get philosophical.

REG
Why?

GROVER *(curt)*
Why?
Because it's a drag That's why.

REG
Well I feel different.
Ever since I stopped drinking
it's like a fog lifted and I
can see clearly.

GROVER *(gimlet-eyed)*
You never stopped drinking.
You were drinking this morning //

REG
I had one bloody drink *Jesus*!
(tries to recover)
Life is diverse and there are
diverse experiences of it
diverse energies
it's a lot happening.
Sometimes it's overwhelming
but it's not *ugly*.
(beat)

Life isn't ugly I *know* that
even though it seems ugly on the surface
sometimes—or even most of the time
but that's a surface.
You peel back the surface and—
I'm reading Carlos Castaneda right now
you ever read him?

GROVER
No

REG
He writes that the great sin
The biggest sin of all
Is to believe that life itself is not good.
Whether in failure or success
we must never take our eyes from the fact
that it is an amazing world
and we must rise to its challenges.
And we must love life.

GROVER *(a real question)*
Is that something you can do?

Reg turns to look at him.

Grover, Charlie, and all members of the band file in. Diana sits far away from Peter.

SIMON
So
let's have our little meeting shall we?

Everyone clusters around.

SIMON
So I went down to Columbia
With our new producer Mister Grover.
(everyone applauds, says "woo Grover," etc.
Grover blushes and sips his beer)
Do you want to tell them?

GROVER
Good news.
Columbia loves the two songs
They're ecstatic.

HOLLY
That's great.

SIMON
They think that either can be a lead single—

PETER
Let's not talk about singles.

SIMON
What would you like to talk about, Peter?

PETER
That's commercial bullshit
I don't care about that shit.

SIMON
I'm just relaying what Columbia wants us to know.

PETER
I mean it's great but
I want to talk about the album and
where we are with the album;

we're in the homestretch
I mean I think we are and
there's too much.
We can't fit everything.
I know no one wants to cut anything and
we've talked a whole lot about continuity
But
I'm sorry
We need to have this conversation
We need to decide what we're gonna do;
we're four minutes over
and it's not enough for a double album.

SIMON
Columbia doesn't want a double // album

PETER
Well it's not enough—to—
I'm saying we *can't* do a double album
but it's too long for a record.

SIMON
Right //

PETER
We need to cut stuff //

SIMON
I misunderstood you.

Pause.

REG
Why can't we do a double // album?

DIANA
I know where this is going
and I'll tell you right now—let's just
cut to the chase
I am not cutting whole verses out of my songs
I am not budging on that particular issue
So let's rethink—*reframe*—how we're
going to have this conversation—

SIMON
Who said anything // about

DIANA
Because—and I know we all want
the same thing No Simon because
I know where this is going—

SIMON
But //

DIANA
but I am not mutilating what
I wrote
I'm sorry
I'm just not
So
we need to reframe this whole way of thinking
about what to do with the album
because it's not
falling on my shoulders because
I won't let it.
(uncomfortable quiet)
We need to come together in
a different way or I'm walking
out the door.

PETER
Well something needs to go //

DIANA
Well then something needs to go
I'm not // arguing that

PETER
You just // said

DIANA
I'm just *telling you* where
I'm drawing *that* particular
line.
That's it.
That's all I'm doing.

Pause.

SIMON
Not to be niggling but
you have more songs than anyone else
You have five songs on this album.

DIANA
So what?
What does it matter // if I

SIMON
It's a matter of real estate
that's all.
"Bright" is right now at 6:38
It's the longest song on the album.

DIANA
So cut it.

SIMON
I'm // just

PETER *(to Diana)*
Is that what you want to do?

DIANA *(laughing)*
Is that what *I* want to do?
No that's not what I want to do but
you're putting me in an impossible
position. And I was not prepared
to have this conversation
because I thought we were going to
talk about Columbia.
I was busy being nervous about
Columbia and what they
thought of the songs
and now you're springing this—whole
other *thing*.

Pause.

HOLLY
Or we could cut one of my songs
Or one of Peter's.

PETER
We've already cut "Seven Roads" and
"Masquerade"

DIANA
And "Domino"
And "Lay in Your Arms"

Beat.

SIMON
There are thirteen songs to choose from
But Peter is right
We need to cut four minutes from the album
I don't know how to do it but
That is a fact.

Pause.

GROVER
I think you guys should all sleep on it
And let's take a look at it in a couple of days.

SIMON
Okay.

PETER
Okay.

GROVER
Everyone else good with that?

Pause.

GROVER
See you in a couple of days.

REG
Do we have any ideas about album titles?

They all look at him.

REG
Because two nights ago Paula had a dream we called the album "Mudfuck"

And she said the cover had a picture of
a girl on a dinosaur with mud on her
Wearing a loincloth
sort of prehistoric.
I don't know what it means.
(pause)
I just thought I would say it.

Weird silence.

GROVER
Okay
well
let's . . . all talk about it later.

Simon laughs quietly to himself.
Grover exits into the sound room
and disappears out of sightlines.
Everyone else scatters into groups
and leaves the studio piecemeal.

Peter eyes Diana—he's about to
approach her.

Instead, he does a volte-face—he
turns and walks out of the studio.
The studio empties out but for Holly
and Diana.

DIANA
Was I being a complete bitch?

HOLLY
I completely understand where
you're coming // from

DIANA
Be honest with me.

HOLLY
No. You weren't a bitch.

DIANA
I just don't want them
thinking . . .
Well you know how those
boys are.

HOLLY
You're standing up for yourself
It's what you have to do.

Pause.

DIANA
I'll just cut the whole song.

HOLLY
I don't think you // should

DIANA
I mean if it comes down to
that No I will
Simon's right, I have more songs
than anyone else.
And I can just use it on some
other album.
(pause)
Can I tell you something?

Grover reemerges, overhearing them.

HOLLY
Uh-oh
What.

DIANA
No it's good.
(she clasps Holly's hands)
They're giving me a solo album.

Holly's expression slowly changes.

DIANA
I mean, if I want it.
I had a meeting with the suits last week.
(beat)
If anything it would be more of a side thing.

HOLLY
You're leaving.

DIANA
I'm—
no no I'm not leaving the band, I just don't want to say anything yet.

She waits for Holly to respond . . .
Waits . . .

DIANA
I shouldn't have told you.

HOLLY
No you shouldn't have.

Pause.

DIANA
Please be happy for me
Please
be happy for me we can't be
in a fight.

HOLLY
I am happy for you.
I'm just sick of all this shit.
(pause)
It's a torture to need people.

DIANA
I'll call you.
(beat)
Maybe // we can

HOLLY *(curt)*
I'll see you in a few days.

DIANA *(feeling awful but covering)*
Okay.

Holly very suddenly hugs her,
holds her very tight, lets her go, and
quickly exits.

Diana stands there for a minute.
She notices Grover. They lock eyes.

DIANA *(to herself)*
Jesus Christ . . .

Diana realizes the talkback is on.
She sighs despondently.
Shuts off talkback on the console.

Grover simultaneously turns off the lights in the sound room.

Grover enters the control room.

DIANA
Did you just hear every word of that?

The darkness in the sound room creates a mirror effect against the glass window, duplicating their image.

GROVER
Listen, I get it
Okay?
You do what you have to do
That's
the business.
Everyone's looking out for themselves.
It's Hollywood.

DIANA
Hollywood Are you . . . ?
No That's—Why would you say that to me?

GROVER *(taken aback)*
What?

DIANA *(pleading)*
Grover *no.*

GROVER
What do you mean no?

DIANA
Don't get these stupid ideas
in your head, okay?
Don't turn into one of these people.

Grover looks away, ignominious.
A beat.

DIANA
I'm not leaving the band.

GROVER *(chastened)*
I'm . . . sorry, I didn't // mean to

DIANA
It's okay.
I'm just
You took me by surprise just now.

GROVER
Sorry.

DIANA
It's fine.

Pause.

GROVER *(reticent)*
But . . . don't you think this was . . .
kind of
like
a *nightmare*?

Diana looks at him, it's very serious—but she can't contain her laughter.

GROVER *(PTSD)*
No but I mean really.

DIANA
Honestly? This was the best thing
that ever happened to me.

She shrugs.

GROVER *(volte-face)*
Right. I didn't mean to // offend you just

DIANA
But I know what // you're saying

GROVER
Oh—*yeah*

DIANA
I // didn't

GROVER *(proleptic apology)*
What? Oh *no*—I know!

DIANA
I was // just

GROVER
Yeah. *No.*
Yeah I get it.
(beat)
And I really
Yeah and I feel like I
grew a lot.

It's awkward.

GROVER
I mean more professional.
On a professional level.

DIANA *(not knowing how to respond)*
Oh
Okay.

Beat.

GROVER
And anyway . . . there's nothing else I could do.
I mean with my life. Like
where would I go? It's not like I have a choice.

DIANA
But
I mean we all have a choice—

GROVER
Yes I have a choice
you always have a choice
but that's not what I mean
I just
(the veneer starting to crack)
It just hasn't been that
easy
for me.

Diana looks at him with a tiny bittersweet smile.
She fixes a stray hair on his head.

DIANA
What are you working on after this?

GROVER
I'm doing an album with Hall & Oates.

DIANA *(surprised)*
Really?

GROVER
Yeah.

DIANA *(dryly disappointed)*
Okay, if that's what you want.

Grover busts out laughing. Diana laughs.

GROVER
You don't like Hall & Oates?

Diana mimes locking her lips with a key and throwing it away.

GROVER *(singing from "Sara Smile")*
"Baby hair"

DIANA AND GROVER
"With a woman's eyes
I can feel you watching in the night"

GROVER
"If you wanna be free-eeee . . ."

DIANA
You have a good voice Grover.
(he gives her a look—like, whaa?)
He's actually a really nice person.

GROVER
Daryl?

DIANA
He's a sweetheart.

GROVER
Yeah that's what I hear.

Pause.

GROVER
I never really engineered for The Eagles.
(pause)
I lied, basically.

Beat.

DIANA *(smiling)*
Oh baby, we all knew that.

GROVER *(gobsmacked)*
You did?

DIANA
We knew it before we hired you.

GROVER
So why did you hire me?

DIANA
Well, nobody wanted to.
(beat)
Peter pushed for you.

Grover's expression changes. He gets very still.

GROVER
Peter did.

DIANA
He had an instinct about you.
Peter has good instincts.

Pause.

GROVER
I didn't know that.

Diana checks her watch.

DIANA
You wanna walk me to my car?

GROVER *(still very shaken)*
I'm gonna do a little more over here.

DIANA
Okay baby.
Don't work too hard.

GROVER
Okay.

DIANA
I'll see you.

GROVER
See you.

She exits.

Grover stands for a moment.
He takes a single shuddering breath.
The studio feels eerily empty.

He sits at the console and plays
"Drive"—Holly's song we heard in
the beginning of the play,
but newly arranged, more finished.
He pulls out instruments with the faders
one by one until
We just hear the drums.
He slowly moves the levels so
that the music fills it in again.

Then slowly the vocals come back.

He rewinds. Plays back.
Pulls out everything but the harmonies
And the track of disembodied vocals—
the ones from the top of the act
returning as ghostly echoes.

Then he pulls out the vocals
and it's just harmony.

Angels.

Blue skies.

SPECIAL THANKS

Stereophonic is a play about partnership, so it makes sense that many people helped to make it happen over the course of the decade I spent writing it.

The play would not be what it is without the incredible largesse and artistry of everyone at New Dramatists—in particular Emily Morse, who encouraged me to workshop a play for three weeks when I had not a single word written. Thank you to the director of that workshop, Adam Greenfield, and to the extraordinary set of actors who participated: Mike Shapiro, Gayle Rankin, Alex Hurt, Rebecca Hart, Thomas Jay Ryan. Your hearts and souls are woven into this play.

Thank you too to the frighteningly talented actors who gave their time and energy to developing the play in numerous workshops: Susannah Flood, Will Harper, Alexandra Socha, Chris Sullivan, Theo Stockman, Louisa Krause, Molly Ranson, Stark Sands, Michael Esper, Will Brill, Blake DeLong, Andrew Butler, Shane

Chapman, Sarah Tolan-Mee, Alex Breaux, Sarah Hunt, Patch Darragh, Marianne Rendón, Gabriel Ebert, Benj Mirman, John Kroft, Gideon Glick, Colby Minifie, Lola Kirke, Colin Bates, Nick Selting, Noel Allain, Patrick Vaill, Cristin Milioti, Kim Blank, Gus Halper, Danny Wolohan, Laura Dreyfuss, Matthew James Thomas, Damon Daunno, Carla Duren, Bobby Moreno, Nicholas Braun, Paulina Singer, Christopher Sears, Marin Ireland, Matt Bittner. And of course, to the incredible passel of actors who originated these roles at Playwrights Horizons (and then on Broadway): Chris Stack, Andrew Butler, Will Brill, Sarah Pidgeon, Tom Pecinka, Eli Gelb, and Juliana Canfield. And three geniuses who stepped in for the extension: Amy Forsyth, Rebecca Naomi Jones, Benjamin Anthony Anderson.

THE BAND

To the extraordinary Daniel Aukin, who committed to a loose idea, then stuck with me and a very inchoate series of pages for years on end and believed it could be a play.

To my gentlemanly composer Will Butler, who trusted me unconditionally and who made this play sing—in all ways.

To the nonpareil of all music arrangers and one of the best humans alive, Justin Craig.

To sound engineer and guru John Kilgore, who gave me the skinny on everything to do with engineering and producing records.

To our wildly creative sound designer Ryan Rumery, who showed me all the ways technical screw ups could be dramatic gold.

To all the people who assisted me—Wesleigh Gates, Sam Theobald, and Laura Dupper—and most especially to Julia

Greer, whose dramaturgy and insight show up everywhere in these pages. *Stereophonic* would not be the play it is without her incisive contributions.

MY PALS

To Raphael Martin for his stalwart efforts in forging crucial relationships.

To Sarah Benson, Jon Dembrow, and everyone at Soho Rep., who developed the play in its initial phases.

To Philip Himberg, Janice Paran, Christopher Hibma, Ignacia Delgado, and everyone the Sundance Theatre Lab, for being the perfect stewards of new play development. Thanks as well to Ayad Akhtar and Lynn Nottage for their incisive dramaturgy and endless collegial kindness.

To P. Carl, Jamie Gahlon, and the Mellon Foundation, without whom this play wouldn't exist.

To Joy Meads and everyone at Center Theatre Group—who commissioned and developed *Stereophonic* in several crucial (and expensive) workshops. Thank you for believing in me. Thanks as well to Kelley Kirkpatrick and to Second Stage Theater.

To Adam Greenfield for more than I can say, and to everyone at Playwrights Horizons.

To my uber-agent Emma Feiwel for staying the course and cheering me on when I couldn't see a way forward.

To my lawyer Ira Schreck, a genuine mensch and a true friend.

Thank you to Yaddo, The MacDowell Colony, the Bogliasco Foundation, Millay Arts, American Academy in Rome, the Dora Maar House/Brown Foundation. And to Michael Mekeel, Fran Offenhauser, Jim McCarthy, and Gloria Peterson for old-school patronage.

To Paul Rusconi, Nate Heiges, Larry Rand, Jonathan Fuchs, Mindy Walder, Ann Marie Healy, Anne Washburn, Gordon Dahlquist, Gaby Calvocoressi, Angeline Shaka, Cusi Cram, Peter Hirsch, Melissa Febos, Jo Lampert, Matt Wolf, Rachel Weisz, Olivia Laing, Lucas Hnath, Sheila Callaghan, Tory Stewart, Jen Haley, Kath Tolan, Sibyl Kempson, Sarah Ruhl, Kirsten Greenidge, Heidi Schreck, Kip Fagan, Duncan Riddell, Carol Ireland, Elizabeth Franco, Rachel Aedan, Nancy and Eddie Adjmi, Jordan Harrison, Talene Monahon, Amrita Ramanan, Sarah Lunnie, Liliana Padilla, Hilton Als, Leland Cheuk, Gigi Buffington, Sigrid Nunez, Bella Brodski, Rebecca Taichman, Katie Kitamura, Marie Bshara, Brett Neveu, Diane Cook, Alice Tuan, Sarah Baley, Cory Hinkle, Jen Silverman (and countless others I am surely forgetting!) for their enduring friendship, love, strength, and patience.

Theatre Communications Group would like to offer its special thanks to Julie Morris for her generous support of the publication of Stereophonic *by David Adjmi*

Julie Morris is a member of the PlayMakers Advisory Council in Chapel Hill, NC, and a founding member and co-chair of The Women's Point of View Leadership Council. She serves on TCG's National Council for the American Theatre.

Other TCG books sponsored by Julie Morris include:

Becky Nurse of Salem by Sarah Ruhl

Theatre Communications Group's mission is to lead for a just and thriving theatre ecology. Through its Core Values of Activism, Artistry, Diversity, and Global Citizenship, TCG advances a better world for theatre and a better world because of theatre. TCG Books is the largest independent trade publisher of dramatic literature in North America, with twenty-one Pulitzer Prizes for Best Play on its book list. The book program commits to the lifelong career of its playwrights, keeping all of their plays in print. TCG Books' authors include: Annie Baker, Eboni Booth, Nilo Cruz, Jackie Sibblies Drury, Larissa Fast-Horse, Athol Fugard, Jeremy O. Harris, Quiara Alegría Hudes, David Henry Hwang, Michael R. Jackson, Branden Jacobs-Jenkins, The Kilroys, Tony Kushner, Young Jean Lee, Tracy Letts, Lynn Nottage, Dael Orlandersmith, Suzan-Lori Parks, Sarah Ruhl, Stephen Sondheim, Paula Vogel, Anne Washburn, and August Wilson, among many others.

Support TCG's work in the theatre field by becoming a member or donor: www.tcg.org